Dedication

To my Lord and Savior Jesus Christ Who is my counselor and closest friend, the author and finisher of my faith, and the real author and finisher of this book.

And
To my wife, my sweetheart and the next closest friend, Lilli, whose unselfish love and constant encouragement prayed me through the many long hours of research and writing.

And
To our wonderful children: Tania, Andrei, Anthony and Michael whom we love more than words can tell. Also to their wonderful spouses: Paul, Thea, Alyssa and Ina.

And
To our beautiful grandchildren: Lilly, Sonia, Brayden, Avayah, Xavier, Zander, and Aria.

"God is faithful, through Whom you were called into fellowship with His Son, Jesus Christ our Lord "
1 Corinthians 1:9

TABLE OF CONTENTS

    • Branitski Ancestors
    • SGA "Reflections" Article
    • U.S. State Department Letter
    • Contact Information

Chapter 1   GOD'S PROVIDENCE

"For Thou didst form my inward parts; Thou didst weave me in my mother's womb. I will give thanks to Thee for I am fearfully and wonderfully made; Wonderful are Thy works, And my soul knows it very well" Psalm139:13,14. As I am putting my thoughts together for this book, I will never stop wondering how much the Lord God knew me, loved me and, subsequently, led me into a close relationship with His Son Jesus years later. As King David said, "Such knowledge is too wonderful for me; it is too high, I cannot attain to it" Psalm 139:6.

The title of this book was not chosen by chance. The hateful, deceitful, and corrupt Soviet Union today invokes a sense of disgust. Much has been learned from documentary archives, books and films about the monstrosity of the communist regime.

There was a time, however, when the general public, indoctrinated from an early age, genuinely believed in the precepts of communist ideology, even though their own family members and friends suffered greatly under the evil system.

The wise King Solomon once stated that "there is a way which seems right to a man but it's end is the way of death" Proverbs 14:12. The first 27 years of my life I spent in the Soviet Union thinking that "my ways" were right.

I was born in Kyiv, Ukraine in 1948. Ukraine became a separate, sovereign, independent, democratic country in August of 1991 after the disintegration of the former Soviet Union. At that time the spelling of the capital city changed from the Russian spelling Kiev to the Ukrainian spelling Kyiv.

Both my parents were ardent members of the Communist Party of the Soviet Union. My father, Serafim

Ksenafontovich Branitski (1905-1953), whom I don't remember very well, died of complications from thyroid surgery at the age of 48 when I was only five years old. He had been an honored career officer, seeing combat in both the Russo-Finnish War and World War II. The Red Army's disastrous 105 day war against its Nordic neighbor Finland started in the winter of 1939. The Finns inflicted 300,000 casualties on the Red Army and destroyed tons of material and much of Russia's military reputation. That war, like the assault on Poland, was a direct result of Stalin's nonaggression pact with Hitler. My father was in charge of the regiment of the legendary "Katyusha" self-propelled rockets, and went all the way to Berlin in 1945. He was a colonel in the Red Army, in the Corps of Engineers, with a PhD in military fortification structures.

My father was a highly decorated officer. We still have a number of his orders and medals of valor and courage.

My father, Serafim Ksenafontovich Branitski (1905-1953)

4

Serafim

The ancestors on my father's side go back to Count Franciszek Ksawery Branicki (Polish spelling of Count Francois-Xavier Branitski 1731-1819). In the Addendum at the end of the book I give a small history of my Branitski ancestors.

Count Xavier Branitski (1731-1819)

Chapter 2 MY LIFE IN THE FORMER SOVIET UNION

My mother, Lyubov Isaevna Branitski (1918 - 1997), was a Party instructor at both Kyiv GORKOM (City Council) and Kyiv OBKOM (Regional Council) levels. She later became the High School Principal of the prestigious Central School #48 in Kyiv. This was the school where children of the Communist elite studied. She was only 35 years old with two small children, my half brother Vadim age 13 and me age 5, when my father passed away in 1953. Needless to say that toughened her up being a widow with two active boys.

She was a loving, dedicated, sacrificial and very encouraging mother but she was also a strict disciplinarian when her boys were out of line (and that, I was told, happened frequently). In Proverbs 22:15 it says that "Foolishness is bound up in the heart of a child; the rod of discipline will remove it far from him." Well, my mom used the unscriptural belt instead.

Classmates from School #48 elementary grades (I am second row, far right)

At my mom's school where I also studied there were a number of wonderful Jewish teachers. My first teacher, whom I had from the first to fourth grade, was Izya Mikhailovna Torzhevskaya. She was a wonderful woman and a caring educator who knew how to encourage and bring out the best in her students. I simply adored her. After finishing fourth grade I entered the prestigious Kyiv Suvorovite Military Cadet School at the age of 11 (now called Ivan Bohun Young Cadet Military School). I wanted to be a military officer just like my father. At "Kadetka", as the school was customarily called, a number of subjects were taught in English which came in handy later on. The discipline was brutal; we woke up at 6:30 AM, went through marching drills, and had a full day of instruction.

I had a good voice and was often called to the office of the Headmaster, Major General Boris Semenovich Kibardin, to sing his favorite Vistula River song. You see, the General fought and was wounded at Vistula River (the longest and largest river in Poland). He often got emotional remembering the events of World War II. He would customarily have a couple shots of Armenian cognac as I was asked to repeat several stanzas of the song over and over again. I will never forget the song as long as I live. Years later his son, Sasha Kibardin, gifted to me a collection of Soviet uniforms purchased from the widows of generals and

officers who were friends of the Kibardin family. I should mention that I didn't last long at Kadetka which was too regimented for my liking.

Years later I had the opportunity to speak at the same military school that I had attended as a boy.

I returned back to my School #48 where my mom was the principal. The majority of my school teachers were Jewish. My mother was summoned to the City Department of Education (GORONO) several times where she was criticized for having, as they put it, "a non-indigenous teaching staff," *(не коренные учительские кадры)*, to which she would strongly reply "I have the best teachers in the city and entire Kyiv region and am not about to change it any time soon." Now, remember that previously my mother was a Communist Party instructor and she had a few influential friends high up in the Party ranks. That is why she ignored the GORONO suggestions. Any other principal would have been intimidated. Needless to say, my mother, being Ukrainian, was highly respected by the Jewish staff and students alike. Those who later immigrated to Israel on Jewish visas sent her letters of gratitude for sheltering and protecting "this non-indigenous Jewish staff."

With my mother, a strict Director of School #48

8

My first piano teacher was Sara Shapiro who taught me how to play and appreciate music. I was seven years old at the time. I vividly remember how I would memorize the piano piece and play it without turning the music sheets. She would always remark, "Vitya, don't forget to turn the page!" realizing that I was not reading the notes. My music lessons lasted for less than a year and I started to gradually forget the music notes and continued playing by ear. We had a piano at home and I enjoyed playing and improvising. Now, of course, I wish I could read sheet music.

Approximately at that time I started playing soccer on a junior team for the famous Dynamo Kyiv Soccer Club. As a youth team we won several All-Union competitions and in 1975 the team won the UEFA European Championship.

When I was a student at Kyiv State University I was invited to join a rock group named "SADKO" (named for a mythological Russian merchant and traveling musician who fell in love with the daughter of the Slavic equivalent of Neptune). They needed a keyboard player and vocalist, and I gladly agreed. We soon became very popular and participated in the first Rock Competition in 1967 held at Kyiv Central Post Office Auditorium called "The Seventh Heaven." Our lead guitar was Sasha Stetsenko, who was born in Belgium of Ukrainian immigrant parents. His parents later immigrated back to Ukraine following Stalin's propaganda and promises of a good life. Sasha spoke native French and among other songs sang Salvatore Adamo's hits that were very popular in the USSR.

Our rhythm guitar and vocals was Misha Fedoseev, who was born in Glasgow, Scotland. His parents brought him to Ukraine as a teenager under similar circumstances. English was his native language and he sang like Paul McCartney.

Bass guitar was Valera Anureev and our drummer was Volodia Zybin. Volodia is my life long friend and currently is my coordinator in Kyiv for Slavic Ministries. Volodia later played for the well-known Ukrainian Concert Music Organization UKRKONTSERT. He certainly was a virtuoso.

We regularly performed at the Eureka Cafe in Pechersk district to overflowing audiences. We sang Beatles, Rolling Stones, The Mamas and the Papas, The Hollies, Trogs, The Everly Brothers and some of our own songs. Tickets to our concerts were hard to get. We also had several appearances on Ukrainian TV and once on East-European television. Those were the days!

Two of my senior Instructors at Kyiv State University were Jewish: Mrs. Kalik and Mrs. Volik. Both were excellent English language teachers who specialized in written translation and oral interpreting

My close friends in Kyiv were from Jewish families. When I would come to see them their grandmas, who spoke Yiddish, would compliment me for not drinking (remarkably in the country where drinking was a national past time I did not drink hard liquor). While scolding and shaming their grandsons for excessive use of alcohol they would lament, "look at Vit'ki, he does not drink, he's a soccer player---A FUTBOLIST! And you! DU BIST SHANDA FUR DI GOYIM (You are a disgrace for the goys!)." To this day I remember their remarkable stories of survival while a number of their family members perished during the Holocaust in Kyiv's Babiy Yar ravine. The massacre took place on September 29-30, 1941. The decision to kill all the Jews in Kyiv (33,771 killed with 29 survivors) was made by East Prussian Nazi district leader Erich Koch; the Nazi Military governor Major General Kurt Eberhard; the Police Commander for Army Group South SS General Friedfich Jeckeln; and the Einsatzgruppe C Commander Otto Rasch, along with the

10

aid of the SD and SS Police Battalions with the Ukrainian Auxiliary Police backed by the Wehrmacht. All of them are now rotting in hell for eternity.

Prophet Zechariah states: "for he who touches you (the Jewish people), touches the apple of His eye" Zechariah 2:8b. Jesus describes hell as "where the worm does not die, and the fire is not quenched" Mark 9:48. To those who rejected Him, Jesus Christ said "In that place there will be weeping and gnashing of teeth when you see Abraham and Isaac and Jacob and the prophets in the kingdom of God, but yourselves being thrown out" Luke 13:28.

My mother taught me early on how to love and respect Jewish people. The story goes how when I was born I was a healthy baby, breastfeeding and gaining weight normally. Then after two or three months I started losing weight because every time my mom would breastfeed me I would spit up the milk. The best pediatricians were consulted to no avail. Mom said I was slowly dying. Unexpected help came from the Jewish Professor of Pediatrics Balaban who lived two apartments down from ours. She told my mom to alternate first giving me a spoonful of cream of wheat, and then breastfeed me and cream of wheat again. That way my stomach would keep the milk and I would not spit up. She was obviously right! Thank you Lord for sending one of your chosen people to save my life.

So, a Jewish professor saved my physical life, a Jewish piano teacher taught me how to play the piano, Jewish teachers pretty much educated me at school and the University, the Jewish Secretary of State, Dr. Henry A. Kissinger, helped facilitate my coming to the United States and joining my American-born wife Lilli (I will share this incredible story later), but it was the King of the Jews Who saved me spiritually for eternity later on. His name is

Yeshua HaMashiach, Ben Elohim - Jesus Christ, the Son of the Most High.

Moved by the Holy Spirit, Apostle Paul, a Jew from Tarsus, when writing to the believers in Rome, stated that "I have great sorrow and unceasing grief in my heart. For I could wish that I myself were accursed, separated from Christ for the sake of my kinsmen according to the flesh, who are Israelites, to whom belongs the adoption as sons and the glory and the covenants and the giving of the Law and the temple service and the promises, whose are the fathers, and from whom is the Christ according to the flesh,who is over all, God blessed forever. Amen" Romans 9:2-4.

The Scripture clearly states that "God has not rejected His people whom He foreknew" and that "there has also come to be at the present time a remnant (Jewish Messianic believers) according to God's gracious choice" Romans 11:2,5. Zechariah, the prophet of the Messianic age, writes that at the Second Coming of Christ "many peoples and mighty nations will come to seek the Lord of hosts in Jerusalem and to entreat the favor of the Lord." Thus says the Lord of hosts, "In those days ten men from all the nations will grasp the garment of a Jew saying, Let us go with you, for we have heard that God is with you" Zechariah 8:22,23.

Psalm 122 encourages believers to pray for the peace of Jerusalem:
"Pray for the peace of Jerusalem:
May they prosper who love you.
May peace be within your walls,
And prosperity within your palaces.
For the sake of my brothers and my friends,
I will now say, "May peace be within you."
For the sake of the house of the Lord our God,
I will seek your good "
Psalm 122:6-9.

The Peace of Jerusalem is "The Prince of Peace" -- Jesus, from Isaiah 9:6 Who is also called "Wonderful Counselor, Mighty God, Everlasting Father, Prince of Peace." Apostle Paul says: "But now in Christ Jesus you who formerly were far off (gentiles) have been brought near by the blood of Christ. For He Himself is OUR PEACE, Who made both groups into one, and broke down the barrier of the dividing wall" Ephesians 2:13,14.

Mother's Father

The story of my grandfather on my mother's side, Isai Yakov Ishanian (1874-1918), turns out to be both sad and tragic. He was a wealthy Armenian merchant who came from Persia to Novospassovka in the Sea of Azov area of Ukraine in 1918. He met my grandmother, Olga Alekseyevna, when she was eighteen. She was fair haired with blue eyes. He was forty-four, handsome, dark complected and rich. Sometimes opposites attract, but not in this case. When Isai asked my grandmother to marry him she was hesitant, I was told. Olga told her father, Aleksei, that she was too young to marry "that old foreigner." Father's answer, "If you don't marry him you will stay single all of your life. You'll be an old maid (*ти будеш на все життя виковухою*). So she reluctantly agreed to marry Isai.

Little did she know, however, what would transpire later and what a blessing in disguise that marriage would be for so many people in her family. My mother told me my grandma Olga's story, describing how Isai rolled out a beautiful persian rug and proceeded to toss down hundreds of pure gold coins, covering the entire carpet with ten ruble Tsar Nicholas II coins asking for my grandma's hand in marriage (current value of this coin is $945.00 each). At that time there was a

13

devastating famine in Ukraine (1918-1920) and Isai single handedly saved the entire family and my grandma's relatives (twenty-two people altogether) from inevitable starvation by feeding them from the tea shop (чайная) that he owned where bread, sausage and other staples were sold.

Bolsheviks started pouring into the Sea of Azov in 1918 and my grandma's family was afraid that Isai might be in danger. So, early one morning, grandma's aunt Nyura covered my grandpa Isai with hay in a horse drawn wagon and brought him to the sea harbor. Grandpa told grandma that the Bolsheviks would not stay in power for long and the plan was to ship him away from Novospassovka for several months...that was the last time my grandma saw her husband alive. My mom was two months old at the time. Locals later told my grandma that very few who were brought to the harbor that day made it to the ship. The NKVD (Secret Police) arrested most of the passengers, confiscated their possessions and shot some on the spot and threw the bodies into the sea. Only the Lord God knows what happened to my grandfather Isai.

The story of my grandfather Isai (Isaiah in English, which in Hebrew means Jehovah is salvation) brings to mind the Biblical story of Joseph (which in Hebrew means may Jehovah add) who saved his family from famine and brought all seventy of them to Egypt: "...all the persons of the house of Jacob, who came to Egypt, were seventy" Genesis 46:27. It makes me reflect on God's remarkable providence and His plan for my life: "For I know the plans that I have for you, declares the Lord, plans for welfare and not for calamity to give you a future and a hope" Jeremiah 29:11. So, had it not been for Isai marrying my grandma Olga, neither my mom nor I would have been born.

My grandma, like my mom, never remarried. Thus my great grandfather Aleksei's prediction for his daughter was sadly fulfilled--from age nineteen to sixty she was single. She worked extremely hard in the coal mines of Stalino (now the city of Donetsk) for over twenty five years.

My grandma lived with us in Kyiv. She complained to my mom that her retirement pension was so small after working so hard in the mines as a coal digger. At some point she even wanted my mom to write a letter to Nikita Khrushchev who, my grandma said, visited her mine in Stalino as a political propagandist in the early 1930s. Grandma was seeking justice. My mom was mortally afraid that it might cause problems at her work and tried to persuade her "to not even think about it." You see, in the country where people were constantly intimidated by the KGB, where friends and relatives could not trust each other out of fear of being branded "unreliable elements" or worse--"enemies of the people" for criticizing the current government, one could understand my mom's uneasiness. It should be noted that my grandma was illiterate so my mom's worries were put to rest...until one fateful summer morning in 1954. After my mother left for work, grandma bribed my older brother, Vadim, with three rubles to write a letter to, you guessed it, Khrushchev himself!

By the time Stalin died in March 1953, Nikita Sergeevich Khrushchev, a skilled Party apparatchik, had positioned himself as a possible successor. Six months later, at the age of 59, he became the most powerful individual in the USSR assuming the position of the First Secretary of the Communist Party of the Soviet Union. Remember the guy? He was indeed a piece of work banging his shoe on October 12, 1960 at the Plenary Meeting of the United Nations in New York in protest after the speech by Philippine delegate Lorenzo Sumulong.

The American media reported, "Khrushchev Brought Chaos to the UN."

Well, a few weeks later our nervous mailman delivered to our door a government (*правительственную*) telegram from Moscow with the very official looking red stripe across it. Here is the text: "Dear Olga Alekseevna! Thank you for your letter and the memory of my visit to your coal mine. I am grateful to you for your selfless labor to the glory of our Socialist Motherland. The record of your working years was found and verified. By the Verdict of the Presidium of the Supreme Soviet of the USSR you are awarded the All-Union pension. Signed Nikita S.Khrushchev."

Now we are talking 550 rubles a month for my grandma who previously was receiving a mere 60 rubles. In comparison my mom was making 350 rubles as a high school principal, and when I was teaching English at Kyiv Institute of Light Industry, after graduating from Kyiv State University, I was making 120 rubles (back then one ruble was equal to one U.S. dollar). There you have it! My grandma certainly was worth every penny of it, or should we say, kopek. She died in 1960 at the age of 60. I remember her as a loving, caring and generous woman. It was my grandma who taught me The Lord's Prayer in church Slavonic and took me as an infant to the famous Saint Vladimir Cathedral in Kyiv to be baptized. My mom told me about it years later and warned me not to tell anyone. In the Soviet Union's atheistic society faith in Christ was ridiculed and banned..

Visiting my grandmother Olga's grave
in Kyiv 2018

My father's grave
at the Kyiv Military
Cemetery

I will tell you later
how I came to the saving faith in Jesus Christ here in

America at the age of 30. Apostle Paul in his Epistle to the church of Rome writes, "Or do you not know that all of us who have been baptized into Christ Jesus have been baptized into His death? Therefore we have been buried with Him through baptism into death, in order that as Christ was raised from the dead through the glory of the Father, so we too might walk in the newness of life. For if we have become united with Him in the likeness of His death, certainly we shall be also in the likeness of His resurrection, knowing this, that our old self was crucified with Him, that our body of sin might be done away with (reduced to inactivity), that we should no longer be slaves to sin; for he who has died is freed from sin. Now if we have died with Christ, we believe that we shall also live with Him, knowing that Christ, having been raised from the dead, is never to die again; death no longer is master over Him" Romans 6:3-9. What a liberating thought--to be resurrected with Jesus by His grace through our faith in Him!

My mother became a member of the Communist party in 1939. Out of fear of being branded as an "unreliable citizen" she had to hide who her own father was and what the Communists had done to him. She taught me early on to say, if asked at school about my grandpa, that he was a miner and that he had died in a mine explosion.

It should be noted that in the former Soviet Union, out of the then 250 million people, only approximately 20 million were actually members of the Communist Party. That affiliation was usually one of convenience, to gain promotions and other special advantages offered to party members.

However, there was a small core of people who were truly committed to the Communist ideology and believed the principles it advocated. That minute part of the country's populace sadly included the Branitski family. Indeed "there is a way which seems right to a man, but it's end is the way of death" Proverbs 14:12. As if to underscore the importance of this verse the wise Solomon repeats it verbatim in Proverbs 16:25!

My father and mother, Serafim and Lyuba

The entire country, including our family, lived under this evil, godless ideology for over seventy years! The Union of the Soviet Socialist Republics, commonly known as the Soviet Union, was formed December 1922 and dissolved in December 1991. It was the first country in the world established on godless Marxist socialist ideology. The former Prime Minister of the United Kingdom, Sir Winston Churchill, characterized socialism as follows: "Socialism is a philosophy of failure, the creed of ignorance, and the gospel of envy, its inherent virtue is the equal sharing of misery." Former Prime Minister of the United Kingdom, Margaret Thatcher, said "The problem with socialism is that sooner or later you run out of other people's money." An old saying in my former land was "the people act as if they are working, and 'they' (meaning the government) act as if they are paying." That is to say productivity was low as a consequence of meager wages.

Back To My Mom

At the end of her life while living with us in America, my mom came to the saving faith in Jesus

Christ. By God's grace she made her decision in time. King David, whose name in Hebrew means "well beloved of God," writes in Psalms: "Wondrously show Thy lovingkindness, O Savior of those who take refuge at Thy right hand" Psalm 17:7. My mom chose to take refuge in the Savior Jesus after about 78 years of unbelief.

In 1996 during Billy Graham's crusade, Lilli and I were privileged to sing in the choir conducted by Cliff Barrows. What a blessing it was to glorify our Savior with over 700 brothers and sisters and see thousands of people coming up front to repent and receive the Lord Jesus. My mom had been in a coma for several months and we went to see her on Easter morning. Her pulse was almost non-existent, eyes closed shut and she was barely breathing. I remember greeting her with the traditional "Khristos Voskres!" - Christ is Risen! I noticed how her pulse started climbing up on the pulse monitor and the nurse who came to check on her said "your mom heard you." She explained to us that hearing usually goes last. The Bible teaches that even the dead will hear the Lord's voice: "Truly, truly, I say to you, an hour is coming and now is, when the dead shall hear the voice of the Son of God; and those who hear shall live" John 5:25. My mother finally realized the answer to "Who has ascended into heaven and descended? Who has gathered the wind in His fists? Who has wrapped the waters in His garment? Who has established all the ends of the earth? What is His name or His Son's name? Surely you know!" Proverbs 30:4.

I praise you Lord Jesus for revealing Yourself to my mother and for answering prayers of so many people. In the Gospel of John we read about the fact that God loves us. "For God so loved the world, that He gave His only begotten Son, that whoever believes in Him should not perish, but have eternal life. For God did not send His Son into the world to judge the world, but that the world should be saved through Him. He who believes in Him is not judged; he who does not believe has been judged already, because he has not believed in the name of the only begotten Son Of God" John 3:16-18.

Mother with my brother Vadim and his ballerina wife, Lirena, whom we were able to bring to America in 1979

Swallow's Nest Castle

In 1950 my father was in charge of VOENPROEKT which was the Military Design Complex of the Kyiv Region Department of Defense. It was under his direct supervision that the restoration of the Swallow's Nest Castle in Yalta, Crimea, was taking place in the years to follow.

Yalta was where the historic Yalta Agreement between President Roosevelt, Churchill and Stalin was signed in February, 1945 at Tsar Nicholas II Livadia Palace.

The Swallows Nest Castle which is located west of Yalta on the southern coast of Crimea was built by

21

Baron Von Steingel between 1911 and 1912 for his ballerina mistress. It is perched precariously on the sheer 130 foot high Aurora cliff. The building is compact in size, measuring only 66 feet long by 33 feet wide. It seems that it was a trend at that time for a man of standing to have ballerinas as mistresses, so the good Baron was keeping in step with trends. In Russian "моя ласточка" or my little swallow, is a term of endearment used to refer to one's sweetheart (Lilli and I use this term often, especially lately, for our beautiful granddaughters).

Swallow's Nest Castle Crimea

The adjacent military sanatorium, "Zhemchuzhina" (The Pearl), was also designed and built by the Military Design Complex of the Department of Defense where my father worked. My mom and I stayed there several times while my dad was still alive. Later in my teen years I stayed at The Pearl sanatorium on the invitation of my father's close friend and comrade in arms, the late two star general Ivan Dmitrievich Zaitsev. His son Dmitrii was my close friend from childhood through our student years at   Kyiv   State   University,   Department   of   Military Interpreters. I have so many wonderful memories of The Pearl and the absolutely beautiful Swallow's Nest.

As a small child my parents were able to send me to a health spa (sanatorium) for privileged children of the Soviet elite class.   I wonder how many of these little children grew up to be highly placed party apparatchiks.

At Yevpatoria Children's Camp 1952 (far right, bottom row)

The Sea of Azov

As a teenager, I had a not so wonderful memory at another sea, the Sea of Azov. The story of me nearly drowning when I was about sixteen years old is surely an example of God's Providence in my life. My mom, using her party connections, sent me to a Pioneer camp where I was supposed to be a swimming instructor. I was a good swimmer all right but my experience was swimming short distances in the Dnieper River. Long distance

23

swimming in the sea was new to me. When I arrived at the camp the former swimming instructor who was born and raised at the sea challenged me to swim with him.

He was seemingly upset with me that I took his spot at the camp. It was early morning when we set out to the sea. The water was calm and it was hazy. We started swimming without saying a word to each other. It seemed like we swam for about an hour into the open sea. When I turned around the coastline was barely visible. We were at least a mile away from the shore. I got frightened and the next thing I knew I got a leg cramp. My first thought was that I was going to drown. It is true that at such a moment a person's whole life flashes before his very eyes. I experienced it. The next thing I saw was a small fishing boat coming from nowhere and the fisherman who approached us started swearing uncontrollably. "What in the heck are you doing swimming that far out?" he said. "Do you even know which direction to swim to get back?" He was right, the haze was getting more noticeable before sunrise. As I now realize, God sent that fisherman (even with foul language) to save our lives. He pulled us both into the boat. It seemed at the time that I had no strength left. As we were going back to shore I realized that I would never have been able to swim back. The distance was much too great.. The other swimmer and I never told anyone what happened to us for fear of what the camp authorities would do. I also never told my mom what happened to me at the Sea of Azov!

Father's Family

My father had four brothers and one sister (Vasily, Nikolai, Yakov, Vladimir and Alexandra). Vasily was the oldest. He was a transportation engineer. His position in 1937 was Kommissar of South West Railroad

24

Transportation. He was one of the eighteen Ukrainian Ministers who was killed in Stalin's Great Purges.

The purpose of the Great Purges in Russia and Ukraine was to eliminate "enemies of the regime and dissidents," by eliminating potential rivals in the ruling elite, to ensure complacency of the terrorized population, to divert attention from the failings of the state and to satisfy Stalin's own sociopathic tendencies. Joseph Vissarionovich Stalin (real name Dzhugashvili), nicknamed "Koba," was indicted for robbery and murder before the Bolshevik October 1917 Revolution. Ruthless and unmerciful, he was guilty of ordering millions of executions (in Ukraine, alone, 170,000 people were executed by 1937-1938). Earlier, during the years 1933-1934, Stalin's induced GOLODOMOR - "to kill by starvation" cost nearly seven million Ukrainian lives. Some historians estimate that this man-made genocidal famine in Ukraine took closer to twelve million lives. Thirty thousand men, women and children were dying daily.

Since 2003, the Golodomor has been recognized as a genocide of the Ukrainian people carried out by the Soviet government. The twenty-five countries of the United Nations declared that seven to twelve million Ukrainians perished. That is how Stalin tried to suppress any opposition, including the Ukrainian independence movement.

Being a Georgian by nationality, Stalin could care less about Slavic people, and by the beginning of World War II over twenty million citizens had perished during his mad purges. He was simply a murderer, killing Communists and rank and file citizens alike. Recently declassified data (2017) disclosed by the Russian Parliament (Duma) estimates Soviet Union war losses at close to forty-two million (war losses recognized by previous Russian presidents had ranged from seven

25

million (Stalin), twenty million (Khruschev), twenty-five million (Brezhnev), and twenty-seven million (Gorbachev).

Uncle Vasily's son, Viktor, whom Lilli and I met in Kyiv during my missionary trips to Ukraine in the 1990s told me the story how in the early fall of 1937 the NKVD (Stalin's Secret Police) came to arrest my uncle Vasily and his family (his wife and three children.) The usual tactic was to come during the middle of the night when people were sound asleep. When the agents tried to forcibly open the door of the apartment, little Viktor, who was six years old, hid under the bed. He caught a glimpse of his father, mother and two sisters being escorted in their pajamas out into the cold to the waiting black police car "voronok." A few hours later the neighbors found the terrified little boy under the bed refusing to come out, shaking and crying. They brought Viktor to the village where another family adopted him and gave him a new last name: Petrov. That is how my cousin Viktor Branitski became Viktor Petrov. Viktor was seriously ill when we met him in Kyiv. I brought him medicine from the United States several times but the disease was progressing. He had an acute form of adenoma and died in 1994.

Viktor was a colonel, a military medical doctor who served in East Germany. He told us horror stories of how political prisoners were treated in the former German Democratic Republic and how medical experiments akin to those performed by Nazi doctors were conducted on them. The survival rate was almost non-existent. The world was not supposed to find out the real truth.

I have Viktor's military uniform at home that he gave me the last time I saw him. I also had a chance to witness to him, his wife, and his son while in Kyiv. I know the Lord Jesus arranged that meeting and believe that someday I will see Viktor Branitski-Petrov in heaven.

26

"Hence, also, He is able to save forever those who draw near to God through Him (Who holds priesthood permanently – Jesus Christ) since He always lives to make intercession for them" Hebrews 8:25.

Uncle Vasily with his younger brother, my father, Serafim

Uncle Vasili's son Dr. Viktor (Branitski) Petrov

CHAPTER 3   SOME HISTORY ABOUT UKRAINE

Religion

In the tenth and eleventh centuries Kievan Rus became one of the largest and most prosperous states in Europe. Vladimir the Great (980 - 1015) and his son,Yaroslav the Wise (1019 - 1054), ruled during this time known as the Golden Age of Kyiv. Vladimir wanted to unite the people under one religion so around 988 he sent envoys to examine the major religions--Islam, Judaism, Catholicism, and Orthodoxy. Vladimir was very impressed by the description of his emissaries of the worship they saw in the great Cathedral of Hagia Sophia in Constantinople: "We knew not whether we were in heaven or on earth, for surely there is no such splendor or beauty anywhere upon earth."   Having heard this account, Vladimir chose Eastern Orthodox Christianity. To this day,   Orthodoxy is the predominant religion in Ukraine. .

St Michaels' Orthodox Church, Kyiv

Some Facts About Ukraine

The former Soviet Union was comprised of fifteen Republics of which Ukraine was the second largest. Territory-wise Ukraine equals the territory of Texas and is the second largest country in Europe after unified Germany. Twenty five years ago Ukraine possessed the world's third largest nuclear arsenal. It had inherited 175 long range ballistic missiles and more than 1,800 warheads after the collapse of the Soviet Union. Following two years of talks between the United States, Russia, and Ukraine, President Bill Clinton announced a breakthrough on January 10, 1994 at a press conference in Brussels.

On December 5, 1994 the Nuclear Non-proliferation treaty was signed by Russian President Boris Yeltsin, United States President Bill Clinton, and Ukrainian President Leonid Kuchma in Budapest, Hungary. Known as the Budapest Memorandum on Security Assurances, the agreement officially dismantled Ukraine's nuclear arsenal. Ukraine had agreed to remove all nuclear weapons from it's soil in exchange for assurances that Russia would respect its sovereignty and territorial integrity. Between 1994 and 1996 Ukraine gave up their nuclear weapons, most of which were transferred from Ukraine to Russia !?!

Soviets used rose gold for major connectors in their ICBMs (Inter Continental Ballistic Missiles). The average amount of gold used per long range missile SS-21 was 40 kilos. Ukraine gave up 175 missiles at the tune of $417 million in current gold price (approximately $2,000 per ounce).

The illegal annexation of the Crimean Peninsula by the Russian Federation in February and March of 2014 was a breach of Russia's obligation to Ukraine under the Budapest Memorandum and in violation of Ukrainian sovereignty and territorial integrity.

It was under Obama's administration that the current nominee for the presidency from the Democrat Party, Joe Biden, told the acting President of Ukraine at the time, Olexandr Valentinovich Turchinov, NOT to defend the Crimean Peninsula stating "STAND DOWN! We will handle it!"

Acting President of Ukraine in 2014 Olexandr Turchinov

Ukrainian Armed Forces located in the Crimea (two military bases and several military detachments) could have easily stood against Russian soldiers who initially numbered 150 troops and 20 military vehicles at Perevalnoe area. It was several days later that the Russians increased the number of their troops to 6,000. But, initially, it was a small contingent of Russian Special Forces. I remember watching Ukrainian Live News in absolute disbelief when Ukrainian soldiers numbering a company of 400 men, led by the colonel, courageously marched toward Russian gunmen who were ready to shoot. The Colonel was holding a military Ukrainian flag.

The Ukrainian soldiers were WITHOUT guns because of the STAND DOWN order initiated by Biden on behalf of Obama.

The STAND DOWN order reminds me of an attack on a US diplomatic annex in Benghazi, Libya on September 11, 2012. That day U.S. Ambassador Christopher Stevens and three other American heroes, including two former U.S. Navy SEALs, Tyrone Woods and Glen Doherty and Information Officer Sean Smith were killed by Muslim extremists. They never received life saving help because of the STAND DOWN order coming from the Obama, Biden and Hillary Clinton White House.

When Ukrainians asked for defensive lethal weapons to protect themselves from Russian tanks, the Obama Biden administration only offered blankets. Ukrainians lost over 14,000 military soldiers and civilians and over 22,000 have been wounded and disabled in Russia's war on Ukraine. Donetsk and Lugansk regions have been overtaken by the Russian aggressors who have a concealed Russian military presence there. In contrast to the Obama administration, President Trump supplied Ukraine with Javelin anti-tank missiles which deterred further Russian aggression. The Kremlin organized non-stop propaganda to the local Ukrainian population of the above regions, offering them Russian citizenship.

Another lapse in judgement regarding Ukraine can be demonstrated by Joe Biden's involvement with Ukraine when his son Hunter was serving on the Board of Directors of Ukraine's largest gas producer, Burisma, in 2014 and making over $82,000 a month. The elder Biden, being Vice-President at the time, threatened to withhold $1 Billion in U.S. aid to Ukraine if they did not fire a prosecutor looking into the gas company and his son's dealings. The prosecutor, Viktor Shokin, was ousted in March of 2016 at Biden's request. Shokin was Ukrainian Prosecutor General at the time. So, who, exactly, is guilty of Quid Pro Quo of which Democrats tried to accuse President Trump? Democrats wanted to impeach him from day one of his presidency. With the assistance of the liberal media, they initiated a campaign against a duly elected President and the 63 million Americans who voted for him. How many more millions of American taxpayers' dollars are going to be spent on the endless impeachment inquiries and probes? So far it is 35 million and counting... It sadly reminds me of the Soviet Union's methods of intimidation and manipulation.

Ukrainian demonstration Independence Square, Kyiv

Ukraine declares independence August 24, 1991

Near Independence Square with Ukrainian soldier just back from the battle front, September 2018

Chapter 4   MEETING LILLI

In the beginning of September 1970 a good friend of mine, Valera, invited me to go with him to Crimea. "Let's go for two weeks and dunk our feet in the Black Sea, " he said. The trip involved riding on his K-750 motorcycle which was the most powerful bike in the USSR at that time. We are talking FAST. I jumped at the opportunity and the next day, early morning, we set out on our journey. And, no, I didn't tell my mom where I was going and certainly did not mention the motorcycle. My plan was to call her after we arrived in Crimea. Ukrainian mothers are notoriously known for being overprotective.   In my mother's case it was an understatement.

I was wearing a pair of brand new Levi's blue jeans to be in vogue (back then it was next to impossible to get authentic American jeans). Everything started out great-- beautiful sunshine, moderate traffic but then out of nowhere it started raining real hard. I asked Valera to stop the bike because I was worrying about my newly acquired, should I mention, expensive Levi's blue jeans. As he started braking on the oily highway he lost control of the bike and the next thing we knew we were sliding on the road for at least 25 to 30 feet. The bike was skidding in front of us. It had to be the good Lord Who protected us from the oncoming traffic. When we finally stopped sliding the first thought I had was that I ruined my jeans. (Never mind that we could have been killed).   As I examined the back of my jeans I realized that the only thing missing was my right back pocket, it was sheared off. It was as if it was never there in the first place. So you might safely say that Levi's saved my butt--literally! All these years I promised my kids I would write to the Levi's company to describe my experience, but I never did. I was unscathed but my friend Valerie hurt his elbow badly. Nevertheless, we got to our destination and had two weeks of sheer fun in the sun.

The reason I'm telling you all this is because when we came back from Crimea I met the love of my life, Lilli, in Kyiv. Here is how it happened. My good friend Gennady, with whom I studied at Kyiv State University, and I decided to have lunch at the Dnipro Intourist Hotel. For one ruble we could order a nice lunch (as a student my stipend was 35 rubles a month while Genna, who had excellent grades, received 42 rubles). Genna and I were co-chairs of the English Drama Club at the University of Kyiv. We both loved the English language. He spoke British English while I was leaning toward American English. Until this very day I remember Genna's voice in "The Snows of Kilimanjaro" by Ernest Hemingway that we staged at the university. Our production was a great success.

At the hotel restaurant we were seated at a large table. We were about to order lunch when the hostess seated two more people at our table. They were foreigners, a mother and daughter from the US (no, it was not Lilli yet). Genna and I would habitually practice speaking English, but that time we were a bit shy to speak because the ten year old girl spoke beautiful midwestern American English while her mom spoke with a Ukrainian accent as they conversed. They were from Chicago. We didn't say anything listening to them while they were complaining about the mediocre service from Intourist. We smiled which gave us away that we understood English. Finally, looking at us the girl asked where we were from and for some mischievous reason I said "can you guess?" She and her mom named several countries and finally said "are you from Cuba?" (remember, I had just come back from two weeks in Crimea and had a nice tan so probably I looked like a Latino to her). In the 1960s and 70s Ukraine hosted a number of Cuban students who were admitted to Ukrainian colleges and universities without any entry exams. We were told that communist Cuba and the USSR were comrades-in-arms, you see. I still remember Cuban imported bananas that tasted like soap by the time they got to Kyiv.

Back to our conversation, I told Angelina (she was around 10 years old at the time) and her mom, Zinaida, that I was a Ukrainian and that I was born and raised in Kyiv and that both Genna and I were English language students. Zinaida started crying and told us her story how in 1941, at the beginning of World War II, she was barely 16 when Nazis took her and other young girls from her village to work in forced labor camps in Germany; and how, miraculously, American troops liberated the camp she was in and the next thing she knew she was on her way to America. She was separated from her family and friends who remained in her village in Ukraine. Little did I know, at the time, that my future mother-in-law, Sonia, went through the same horrible experience almost verbatim.

Now, what do you do to console a crying Ukrainian?--champagne! I ordered a bottle of bubbly (that set me back five rubles) and after a few glasses Zinaida calmed down and told us that she had met two young American co-eds on the city sightseeing tour that morning. She said "they are university students from Minnesota and are very cute." She thought we might be interested in meeting the girls. She had bought a watermelon at the local famer's market which she was going to share with the girls that evening and invited us to join them in her hotel room.

Now, at that time contacts with foreigners were, shall we say, highly discouraged (Soviets did not want their citizens to have any contact with foreigners so that they would not hear from them how the rest of the normal world lived. It was the era of the Iron Curtain). Genna and I agreed, nevertheless, to go to Zinaida's hotel room realizing, though, that it might cost us. You see on each floor of the Intourist hotels there were old "babushkas" (grandma-informants) who reported to the administration every step as to who visited which room and when. The plan was to wait one floor down to see if the babushka was away for a bathroom break (knowing how much tea they consumed) and then quickly run up the stairs and enter the room. It worked! As we entered the room, slightly out of breath, we saw Lilli and her friend Kristi for the first time... my heart beats faster as I write this. Lilli was 19, and very attractive. Kristi and Lilli go back several years. They were best friends since high school.

Lilli and Kristi, 1970

When Zinaida introduced us, Lilli asked me where I was from. I was just about to tell her when little Angelina said to Lilli "can you guess?" Lilli also had a hard time figuring it out, guessing that I was from Europe somewhere or possibly from Latin America. Each time she was mistaken Angelina was giggling very cutely. Finally, Lilli said "are you Cuban?" At that point we all started laughing uncontrollably, especially Angelina. I sometimes ask my sweetheart "am I your Cuban?" and get a cute smile in return. I told Lilli that I was Ukrainian. She didn't believe me and decided to check my linguistic skills at which point she asked "вы говорите по русски?"--do you speak Russian? My answer was "yes, I've been speaking it for the past 22 years!" There you have it. She was simply adorable as she tested my language ability.

The Lord Jesus, Whom I did not know at the time, was choosing my future wife for me who would courageously fight for our future together at a time when all hope would seem lost; when Soviets were dead set on declaring me insane and plotting to even kill me. I will tell you our dramatic story later on. The Lord indeed is "mighty to save" Isaiah 62:1.

The next day I invited Lilli, Kristi, Angelina, Zinaida and Genna to our apartment on Pushkinskaya street (which is located downtown Kyiv) for dinner. My mom, who was always very hospitable and whose name was appropriately Lyubov (which means LOVE), cooked a nice Ukrainian dinner which included borsch and varenyki. We all talked a lot and had much fun. Mom talked to Zinaida and listened to her war stories, both of them crying. It seemed to me then that I had known Lilli for a long time, my attraction for her was deepening. Love at first sight you might ask? Yes it was!

Angelina, Genna, Kristi, Lilli, and Zinaida

Lilli was different. She told me she was a Christian, a Baptist. For decades Soviets were persecuting Evangelicals, incarcerating, beating and torturing them for their adherence to their faith in Jesus Christ. Children who were following the Lord in their daily lives were taken away from Christian parents. Churches were destroyed and congregations dispersed. Many evangelicals were exiled to Siberia where they died in harsh conditions. One of many vicious lies that was propagated by the Evil Empire was that Baptists routinely sacrifice their first child to their God. This satanic premise prevails in the country to this very day. No wonder when Lilli told me her family was Baptist I sincerely asked her IF she was the first child and if someone was born BEFORE her. She innocently answered that she was the first born in the family followed by three brothers-- George, Edward and Daniel. (Could I have ever imagined that Lilli and I would some

day have our daughter Tania followed by three boys--
Andrei, Anthony and Michael just like the Sontowski
family)?

So when Lilli questioned why I was persistently
asking her about being the first born in her family I
explained that it was common knowledge that Baptists
sacrificed their first born. Her answer was "You are
NUTS! " I started learning my American idiomatic
expressions. I realized soon enough that nuts are not
only what you eat but that a person could actually be a
nut. I figured out right then and there that I was duped
by Soviet propaganda again.

Talking about sacrifice, the Bible teaches that the
Almighty God, Creator of Heavens and Earth, sacrificed
His One and Only Son Jesus for our sins that IF we
repent of our sins and invite the Risen Savior Jesus
Christ into our hearts WE WILL BE FORGIVEN and will
have ETERNAL LIFE. "FOR GOD SO LOVED THE
WORLD THAT HE GAVE HIS ONLY BEGOTTEN SON
THAT WHOSOEVER BELIEVES IN HIM SHOULD NOT
PERISH BUT HAVE ETERNAL LIFE " JOHN 3:16.

After visiting Kyiv, Lilli and Kristi were supposed to
travel to Kishinev, Moldova, where Lilli's grandmother
and aunt lived. After Kishinev the next stop was to be
Odessa. But In September of 1970 there was a cholera
epidemic banning all travel to Odessa. Lilli sent me a
telegram saying that she was returning back to Kiev. My
mom, rest her soul, did not show me Lilli's telegram and I
was worried that I wouldn't see Lilli again. Finally, a day
before Lilli's arrival to Kyiv my mom showed me the
telegram saying that the train arrives very late in the
middle of the night and that I would never be able to
make it to the train station at that late hour. GET REAL,
MOM!

Genna and I hardly slept that night. We were very
excited at the prospect of seeing Lilli and Kristi again. We

dressed in suits and ties, bought flowers, and hurried to Kyiv train station. Lilli recalls how impressed she was to see us at the station all dressed up. We knew that standard procedure was for an Intourist representative to meet the girls to escort them to their hotel, yet we had hoped that he would be late and we would be the first to meet the girls at the train car. As the train approached I saw Lilli's head sticking out of the window, on her face was an expression of hope of our reunion. Since we were hiding behind the fence so as not to be seen by the Intourist representative, Lilli could not see us whereas we could see her and Kristi. I will always remember her facial expression progressing from being expectant to being dismayed. The train stopped and we rushed to meet Lilli and Kristi at the train car. It seemed like the hug and kiss lasted forever that fateful night at the Kyiv train station. We quickly hopped in a taxi before any Intourist representative arrived. I now know that it was You, Jesus, Who arranged everything.

Meeting Sonia

When Lilli and Kristi left Kyiv in 1970, Lilli stole my heart. She was constantly on my mind and our "love by correspondence" began. In 1971 Lilli's mom, Sonia, traveled to Ukraine and Moldova. The purpose of that trip was to visit Sonia's sister and mother whom she hadn't seen since 1943 when they were separated by the war. It was quite an emotional visit. I remember meeting Sonia in Kyiv before she continued on to Kishinev, Moldova. I never could have dreamed at the time that she would be my future mother-in-law. When in Kyiv I tried to do my very best to impress her. I showed her the sights of Kyiv. We also had several dinners at our apartment during which time my mom enjoyed her conversations with Sonia hearing about her life during the war in the labor camp in Germany and her subsequent new life in America.

My mom and I were just flabbergasted to learn about this remarkable woman's story who, together with her husband, overcame insurmountable difficulties and was able to establish her family in America. She was now visiting the land she had been forced to leave almost 30 years ago. Sonia was a strong believer in Jesus. She gave me my first Bible and shared about how the Lord was with her during all the difficult times in war torn Ukraine and Nazi Germany. I'll never forget how on Sunday Sonia asked to visit an evangelical church. When we got on the city cable car near the train terminal Sonia asked the conductor where the Evangelical Baptist Church was. The conductor, who happened to be a Christian and a member of Yamskaya Evangelical Baptist Church, was so excited to meet a Christian from America that she actually got off the cable car, abandoning it temporarily so she could direct us toward the church. It was so fascinating for me to see a woman with such enthusiasm for the Lord that she left her work place to walk us to her place of worship!

First Church Experience

I will never forget the experience of visiting an Evangelical Baptist Church for the first time in my life. When we entered the church the service was already in progress and the message was from the Gospel of Luke. What I heard from the preacher that morning was the historic account of what happened 2000 years ago in the Roman Empire at the birth of Christ. Now, at the University of Kyiv, among other subjects, there were courses on the history of the Roman Empire. So, when in church I heard names like Herod, the King of Judea; Caesar Augustus, from whom the decree went out regarding the first census; Quirinius, who was governor of Syria, I was really surprised. This information was in our history books. How is it possible that Luke knew all of that? How could he know all of those historic names and events?

The answer was that he received the information from "eyewitnesses and servants of the word" who had handed it down to believers like Luke, who, in turn, "investigated everything carefully from the beginning and wrote it out in consecutive order" Luke 1:3, presenting it to Theophilus. Apostle Luke, "the beloved doctor," was a superb historian.

Sitting in the church I also paid attention to the people who came to worship God. The church was completely filled with hundreds of people. There was not a single empty seat. They sang beautiful heartfelt hymns. I also remember the podium from which there hung a beautiful tapestry embroidered in golden thread stating GOD IS LOVE (БОГ ЕСТЬ ЛЮБОВЬ). I kept looking at that sign thinking that if God is love and I am in love with Lilli, it is a good God, the God of love that I can relate to. The Scripture says "Beloved, let us love one another; for love is from God; and everyone who loves is born of God. The one who does not love does not know God, for GOD IS LOVE" 1 John 4:7,8. That's what it was! I didn't know it at the time.

The two hour church service flew by like 10 minutes for me. When at the end of the service the pastor invited people to convey greetings that people might have from other churches, to my amazement, Sonia stood up and said "I bring you greetings from your brothers and sisters in the United States." That was pretty much the end of the service. People started rushing toward us, hugging and kissing us-- women were kissing Sonia, men were kissing me, ON THE LIPS! They take Apostle Paul literally, you see, "Greet all the brethren with a holy kiss"

44

1 Thessalonians 5:26.   Brothers assumed that since I was sitting with Sonia I was her son and a believer. You might safely say that I was "holy-ghosted" that memorable Sunday at Kyiv Central Baptist Church. Even though I was not quite a believer at that time I really liked the people's sincerity and genuineness. They were true believers in the Lord.

When Sonia and I returned from church we went to our house for dinner and when my mom asked us where we were I didn't even dare to tell her about the church experience.   Back then if you professed faith in Jesus Christ you were risking losing your place of work, your position, or, in my case, expulsion from Kyiv State University.   That fateful meeting in church in 1971 was on my mind for the longest time. In fact, I started telling my closest friends that God exists and He is the God Of Love.

After her time in Kyiv, Sonia continued on her journey to meet with her sister and mother. I can only imagine that meeting in Kishinev. Sonia's sister Tonia and her husband Misha later called me to invite me to visit them while Sonia was there.   It was an unforgettable trip that made me feel like I was part of the family. Sonia told me that "you guys (meaning Lilli and I) should be planning to be together" which gave me amazing hope and affirmation that Sonia was approving of our relationship, and that someday Lilli could become my wife.

Lilli's darling mother, Sonia

Is Our Love FUTILE?

Lilli decided to visit me in 1972. Before that she wrote me a letter stating that she believed our "love by correspondence" seemed like a FUTILE situation to her. I remember reading this letter walking on Lenin street and being quite confused because I did not understand the word "futile." I heard someone speaking American English behind me so I turned around and casually asked them if they could explain the meaning of the word "futile" to me. I told them that I had just received a letter from my sweetheart, Lilli, who lived in Robbinsdale, Minnesota. They almost flipped hearing me mention Minnesota. As it turned out these two men were teachers from Minnesota who were exploring Europe during their summer break. It was Skip Nelson and Jim Van Drunen. They apologetically explained to me the meaning of futile which, obviously, I didn't quite like. So they were very sympathetic and said that when they returned home they would call Lilli and tell her about our meeting and how "wonderful" Victor was. They were my two best advocates. I spent several days with them in Kyiv.

It was my graduation year from Kyiv State University. I invited my newly acquired American friends to my graduation party at Dynamo Restaurant and introduced them to my university professors and friends. I was so proud to have them share that special day with me. Both of them were impeccably dressed for the occasion, Jim wore a white blazer -WOW! It was simply unforgettable. We kept in touch for many years when I came to Minnesota to be with Lilli in 1975. Jim introduced me to his lovely wife Nancy and daughter Karla and I also met Skip's wife Lucinda and family. Both Jim and Skip went to be with the Lord. I will always fondly remember the two teachers from Minnesota that the Lord Jesus sent my way. Both were Christians.

So in 1972 Lilli came back to Kyiv to say goodbye. We spent two weeks traveling together to Leningrad, Moscow, Kyiv, Yalta, Kishinev, and back to Kyiv. Rather than breaking off the relationship we realized that we could not live without each other. Many tears were shed and soul searching done as we tried to imagine our indefinite future. And yet through it all we seemed to have HOPE. Hope that someday things would work out and we would be together. The Scripture says that "Hope deferred makes the heart sick, but desire fulfilled is a tree of life" Proverbs 13:12. The Lord was preparing us for the second part of the verse, testing our resolve to go through insurmountable difficulties and with His divine help to "fulfill the desire" of our hearts."

Lilli and I with Jim and Nancy VanDrunen in Minnesota

The two teachers from Minnesota, Jim and Skip

Chapter 5   HIGH DRAMA

Drama Begins or Scenario Written In Heaven

The Lord God started gradually revealing His plan for Lilli's and my future. In July of 1974, after much prayer and support from her parents, Lilli made the decision to return to Kyiv to marry me. It is easier said than done realizing that Soviet-American marriages were almost nonexistent in the early 1970s. The Soviet bureaucratic machine was doing everything possible to prevent such marriages. What gave Lilli a glimpse of hope was the case of Zhanna and Ronald   Rader. Zhanna was a member of our student theater when she met Ronald, an American Professor from Georgia, who was traveling in Ukraine. They fell in love and decided to get married.

When Ronald came to Kyiv to apply for a Marriage License he was told that he needed "additional documents" from the U.S. in order to marry Zhanna. So he had to do it the hard way, returning back to America several times to get additional documents, each time being informed by the wedding authorities that another legal paper was required. Finally they got married which was no small miracle. Soviets certainly knew how to frustrate unsuspecting innocent Americans.

Ronald and Zhanna

So, it was Ronald who instructed Lilli in Minneapolis as to what legal papers to bring with her to Kyiv. That encouraged Lilli in making her decision. We both are eternally thankful to Ronald and Zhanna for their indispensable advice.

We knew that in order to be married there had to be a thirty day waiting period from the date of application for the Marriage License to the actual wedding day. Lilli ordered her Intourist travel visa having that in mind. She arrived in Kyiv on July 24th and the following day we applied for the Marriage License. We were given the wedding date of August 26th. One of the Intourist travel rules was that you could not be in the same city for more than five days so, to "kill time," Lilli was required to book other cities. She scheduled her tour in such a way that she had to be back in Kyiv from August 24th to 27th so as not to miss the wedding date of August 26th.

I accompanied Lilli during that month to Odessa, Sochi, Sukhumi, Batumi, and Yalta.. She had reservations in Intourist hotels but, being a Soviet citizen, I was prohibited from booking a room in these hotels. I sometimes had to sleep on benches in the courtyards near those hotels. I remember how in Yalta while I was sleeping on the bench, in the middle of the night, a local bum tried to steal my Seiko wrist watch that Lilli had given me. He tried to convince me that it was his watch. I had to physically convince him that he was delusional. I could not wait to see Lilli in the morning after spending nights outside.

When we finally returned to Kyiv August 24, we went to the Wedding Palace (also known as "the Chocolate House" because it was painted in dark brown) with family and friends for our marriage ceremony on our designated date of August 26th. When we arrived we were informed by the Wedding Director, Comrade Stavitskaya, that her office had received a disturbing letter stating that Victor had been treated at several psychiatric clinics in Kyiv. She said that our wedding date was postponed to August 31st or possibly later! This "anonymous letter" was simply a KGB ploy for Lilli's visa to expire so she would have to leave the country. Intourist, of course, refused to extend Lilli's visa.

The Lord knows how we frantically tried to obtain the necessary documents from the psychiatric asylums proving that I had never been a patient there. Lilli's aunt Tonia and her husband Misha came to Kyiv from Kishinev for the wedding that was not to be. They helped us by driving us to various offices to prove my sanity. They were one of the few in the Soviet Union who had a car (which they were able to purchase after being on a waiting list for five years). Misha had been a believer in Communism but his eyes were opened when he saw how our lives were being manipulated by the government.

It was frightening to arrive at the psychiatric clinic at Kurinivka district where Lilli and I needed to obtain the document stating that I had never been treated there. The director of the institution cynically asked me "Victor, are you sure you are not crazy?" He was looking for a bribe which was customary in order to get anything done in the Soviet Union. In order to enter that clinic Lilli and I had to walk through the property where we were surrounded by psychiatric patients roaming about. One old babushka snuck up behind us and hit Lilli with a stick for no apparent reason (probably because she was wearing a mini skirt which was not yet in vogue in Ukraine and deemed to be indecent) ...my poor darling, she went through a lot. Now, looking back we realize that Satan had a diabolical plan for our lives. "The thief comes only to steal, and kill, and destroy" John 10:10a. But the victorious Jesus says "I came that they might have life, and might have it abundantly" John 10:10b.

Clandestine Trip To The American Embassy

A good friend of mine, Kostya Khodos, a sound engineer who assisted our music group on a number of occasions, and his lovely wife Marina, convinced us to go to the American Embassy in Moscow to seek support. "Nothing will be decided in Kyiv, they are trying to trap you. When Lilli's visa expires you will never see her again. This is your ONLY CHANCE. Go and tell the Americans how their citizens are being treated" said Kostya.

Please understand that Lilli was not allowed to go to Moscow without officially pre approved authorization from Intourist authorities. She could not fly without showing her passport and authorization from Intourist. So, air travel was out of the question for her. Taking a huge risk, we chose to go to Moscow by train on August 26th. Again, a passport was needed to purchase a train ticket but we decided to sneak onto the train without a ticket by paying off the train employee. We were determined. We handsomely paid the lady in charge of the train car to sneak us into her private compartment. We told her that Lilli was from Latvia and that she had to be in Moscow to defend academic theses but was not able to get a ticket. Actually, Lilli had majored in Russian at the University of Minnesota and had a good command of the Russian language. She spoke Russian with a slight accent but not an American accent. She sounded like she was from one of the Soviet Baltic countries.

And who was !? I was a university student accompanying her. The train conductor bought our story and agreed to give up her tiny compartment for us for the overnight train in exchange for 300 rubles (the average price for a train ticket back then was 20 to 25 rubles). I remember how Lilli and I held each other tight, fully clothed, barely fitting on that narrow bed. We hardly slept that hot and humid August night with a million thoughts

52

going through our minds. Lilli told me that her family and friends were praying for us. I was afraid to think of the consequences if the Soviet authorities were to arrest me on the way to the American Embassy. Being a military interpreter and first lieutenant in reserves I would be sentenced to ten years in prison automatically. What was a Soviet officer doing at the American Embassy? Subversive activity! Court martial!

Yet realizing that Christians across the ocean were lifting us up to the Lord was a comforting thought and gave us courage and perseverance. U.S. President John Quincy Adams, a devout Christian, is known for his famous words "Courage and perseverance have a magical talisman, before which difficulties disappear and obstacles vanish into air."

The next day we arrived in Moscow, the hustling and bustling capital of the former USSR with its population of seven million (currently 12.6 million). We stayed at a friend's apartment on the outskirts of the city. The Lord gave us a plan as to how to get into the American Embassy since I did not have an American passport to show. You see, every time Lilli would travel to the USSR the front desk of the Intourist hotel would take her passport for a couple days to check her identity. This is standard procedure even to this day. So we thought that if the Soviet security guard at the entrance to the Embassy would ask us for our passports we would say that the passports were left at the hotel.

Also, I thought of using a linguistic trick. I planned to say we were staying at the Rossiya Hotel (the largest hotel in Moscow at the time but currently demolished). My plan was to pronounce the word Rossiya with a heavy American accent using the guttural American "R" versus the rolled Russian "R." Lilli brought me Old Spice deodorant so I smelled American and we agreed that when we approached the Embassy on Tchaikovsky

Street we would tell each other funny stories, laughing and acting as carefree American students. On top of that my American English was getting stronger after talking with Lilli all the time. All of that, we thought, was a recipe for success. And, yes, I was still wearing my well worn Levi jeans and was chewing gum--you guessed it, from the US (there was no gum in the Soviet Union).

As we approached the Embassy a Soviet militia sergeant came out of the glass sentry booth. I was naive to assume that the militia personnel would be country bumpkins with limited knowledge of English. Later at the Embassy we were told that the entire Russian police contingent around the Embassy was actually staffed by highly trained KGB officers, some of them graduates of Moscow Institute of International Relations or MIMO as it is known, where English and other foreign languages were taught.

So, when a tall "sergeant" with an intelligent looking face started walking toward us I got a little nervous. He spoke in good British English and engaged us in friendly conversation, asking what we had seen so far while in Moscow. After the pleasantries we were ready for the inevitable question "may I see your passport please?" I responded in my best American accent "we actually left our passports with the front desk at, you know, Rrrrosiya Hotel down the block." Yep, that's it, it worked! He let us pass through to the Embassy.

At that point it seemed like my knees were locked and for a split second I could not move. Lilli firmly took me by the hand and we were on our way to the Embassy's main entrance. Thank you, dear Lord Jesus for your protection and leading. Looking back I realize that "the effective prayer of a righteous man (and women in Minneapolis) can accomplish much" according to James 5:16b. We couldn't have done it alone without the

54

prayer support from "righteous" brothers and sisters in far away Minnesota.

The distance from the sentry booth to the Embassy's front door was about 70 feet or so. I thought if the "sergeant" would change his mind we would dash to the front door in seconds. Well, he didn't. We rang the bell and when the door opened the first thing we noticed and SMELLED was thick cigarette smoke. That was odd. A young Russian lady asked us in a thick accent "how can I help you?" Lilli told her that we wanted to see the American Council. While we were waiting I noticed that all the clerks who were smoking and typing were Russian women. I was very surprised that the American Embassy employed Soviet citizens who were obviously there to spy and report on what they observed. I thought why would Americans employ these women? Aren't there any bilingual women from immigrant families in the U.S. like Lilli, for example, who would love to do the same work and serve their country abroad?

A tall handsome council dressed in a suit and tie appeared at the door. "Hello," he said "my name is James Huff." We followed him to his office. He had been expecting us since Lilli had called him several times from Kyiv explaining our situation. Of course, the phone conversations were being tapped. Lilli would tell him what was happening in our attempt to get married. As soon as he tried to respond with advice the phone line would go dead.

Mr. Huff sat close to us and motioned to speak softly. The entire American Embassy on Tchaikovsky Street in Moscow was bugged. If that was not enough, Soviets secretly bombarded the Embassy with microwave transmission signals varying between 2.5 to 4 gigahertz. The Moscow Signal, as it came to be known, started in 1953 resulting in an international incident in 1976. The U.S. government determined it to be an open act of espionage. The effect of The Moscow Signal on the American Embassy employees was devastating. Lilli and I learned that another council, Mr. George Fourier, who also helped us, lost his baby in stillbirth as a result of the constant radiation. His family was not alone.

Walter J. Stoessel Jr., U.S. Ambassador to the Soviet Union in Moscow between 1974 and 1976, was among the most effective of American representatives throughout his 40 year career. He died of leukemia in Washington, DC in 1986. He was 66 years old. It was the Ambassador's office that Soviets especially bombarded nonstop for 2 years! What a cowardly shameful act!

On August 29th,1974 Ambassador Stoessel wrote a letter on our behalf to the Department of State, to the Secretary of State, Dr. Henry A. Kissinger who was also the Assistant to President Gerald Ford for National Security Affairs. The letter was classified by the Department of State for 31 years. It was declassified 30 June, 2005. Lilli accidently found it on Wikileaks by entering her maiden name, Sontowski, just a few months ago. That actually prompted my writing this book.

Dr. Kissinger was known for his "shuttle diplomacy." Months before signing the Helsinki Declaration, his office presented Andrei A. Gromyko, Minister of Foreign Affairs of the USSR, the agenda which included policy on emigration and the reunification of families. Our case was included at Ambassador Stoessel's request. I had the distinct privilege of meeting Dr. Kissinger at Amsterdam airport three years ago. Then, at the age of 93, he continued to exhibit sharpness of mind and exceptional memory. Lilli and I thanked him for what he had done for us. Today Dr. Kissinger is 96, bless his heart. Father in heaven, continue to bless this amazing public servant, a true Statesman, American patriot, and a wonderful individual for years to come.

In 1983 I also had the honor of meeting and talking to President Gerald Ford at the IDS (Investors Diversified Services) Key West Florida Retreat. The meeting was arranged by Harvey Golub, then IDS President and CEO. I had the honor of being a member of the IDS President's Advisory Council and Mr. Golub, whose grandparents were from Ukraine, knew my exodus story from the USSR. The Lord allowed me to develop a special bond with Mr. Golub. I remember playing with his baby son at the pool singing "Jesus loves YOU, this I know, for the Bible tells me so." Being Jewish, Harvey and his young wife Roberta knew I was a Christian and were interested in hearing my testimony.

President Ford was the main speaker at the retreat and before he addressed the IDS financial planners I was invited backstage and had the unique opportunity to meet and thank him. He vividly remembered the emigration provision of the Helsinki Declaration regarding unification of families.

Back to our meeting with Mr. Huff at the Embassy. Having heard our story and realizing that Lilli and I had known each other for four years and were serious about getting married, Mr Huff, in our presence, called the Intourist officials and demanded that the Kyiv Intourist branch stop impeding our marriage. The official on the other line assured him that Kyiv Intourist would be notified.

It was lunchtime and Mr. Huff invited us to go to the Embassy's dining room for a hamburger and fries. I enjoyed my first American hamburger with French fries, ketchup, and Coca-Cola. WOW! I will never forget it. Back in 1974 there were no McDonalds in the USSR so for me it was quite a novelty. Mr. Huff gave us special diplomatic train tickets to Kyiv that night (we didn't have to bribe another train conductor) and personally escorted us to the train station.

I should tell you that we drove in a black diplomatic limousine. Another WOW!

The limousine driver was Russian with a very stern look on his face. Again we were bewildered--why not an American driver? We drove in silence knowing that the driver's job was not only to drive but to eavesdrop and report what he had heard. Mr.Huff wished us well and gave us his personal phone number so that we could keep in touch. He was a godsend and we could not thank him enough. For me it was the first taste of official diplomatic America, the country that genuinely cares for its citizens. This initial impression has remained with me to this very day. America is truly a blessed country and "land that I love."

Second Attempt To Get Married At The Wedding Palace

Lilli and I arrived in Kyiv the next morning, August 29th. That afternoon, accompanied by family and friends (should I say fewer friends since a number of them started losing hope that we would ever be married), we headed to the Wedding Palace to be married. At the Palace we explained that we were in Moscow and that the American Embassy had contacted the Intourist officials who confirmed that our case was resolved positively and that we could be officially married. The Director acted as if she had never heard of it and said that she needed additional certificates from psychiatric hospitals to prove that I was not mentally impaired. "It might take several weeks" she added, spitefully. In the meantime Lilli's visa was on the verge of expiring and we were trapped AGAIN! Soviets surely knew how to get on your nerves (вымучить нервы).

Unhappy faces, wedding attempt number two ended in a
resounding rejection--NYET!

We went to the Central Post Office to place a call
to the American Embassy. Every time Lilli would try to
explain our situation the phone would be disconnected
when the Council on the other end tried to speak. It
happened several times. The next day we firmly decided
to go back to Moscow, no matter what. It was the same
scenario, same overnight train, hoping, and in Lilli's case,
praying that this time it would be a different security
guard at the Embassy. I told my mom about our plan.
She was openly crying, saying "son, they will arrest you"
(сынок, они посадят тебя). Now, looking back, I
realize that it had to be Jesus Who was rooting for us and
giving us the conviction to see matters to the end. King
David wrote in Psalm 56, verse 4 "in God, Whose word I
praise, in God I have put my trust; I shall not be afraid.
What can mere man do to me?"

By God's grace everything went smoothly and we
were able to arrive in Moscow safely, go through a

different security guard, and see Mr. Huff again. In our presence he angrily talked to the Ministry of Foreign Affairs official as well as the Intourist Deputy Director and, in no uncertain terms, reminded them that they assured him that they would contact Kyiv authorities to facilitate our case. He also told them that the American Embassy extends the invitation for Lilli to be the official guest of the Embassy or to work at the Embassy "for as long as needed until the bureaucrats in Kyiv received the "necessary documents" from psychiatric hospitals and the couple would finally be married."

While waiting to hear for further instruction from the Embassy, Lilli and I spent several days in Moscow at the apartment of friends of Lilli's aunt Tonia and uncle Misha. We notified Mr. Huff as to where we were for security purposes. We were afraid that the KGB (Soviet secret police) would follow us so we often changed our routes and mode of transportation so as not to be detected. We also checked daily with the Embassy using various public phones to protect our gracious but nervous hosts. The Almighty God kept us safe "He will cover you with His pinions, and under His wings you may seek refuge; His faithfulness is a shield and bulwark" Psalm 94: 4.

Finally Married, But Short Honeymoon

On September 9th we found out from the Embassy that the Wedding Palace in Kyiv was ready to issue us the Marriage Certificate and that same day we went to Kievskiy Vokzal - Kyiv Train Station to catch the overnight train to Kyiv. We were cautiously optimistic. My sweetheart Lilli caught a cold while staying in Moscow and was running a high fever at that time. The constant pressure and mounting hassle of "Soviet hospitality" took a toll on her. The train conductor, a middle aged woman with orange hair who spoke Ukrainian, took pity on us and offered her compartment and tea with lemon and honey.

Arriving early in the morning, September 10th, we went straight to the Wedding Palace in Pecherskiy District.

That morning a telegram was delivered to our apartment on Pushkinskaya Street from Senator Hubert Humphrey. That helped to facilitate our case.

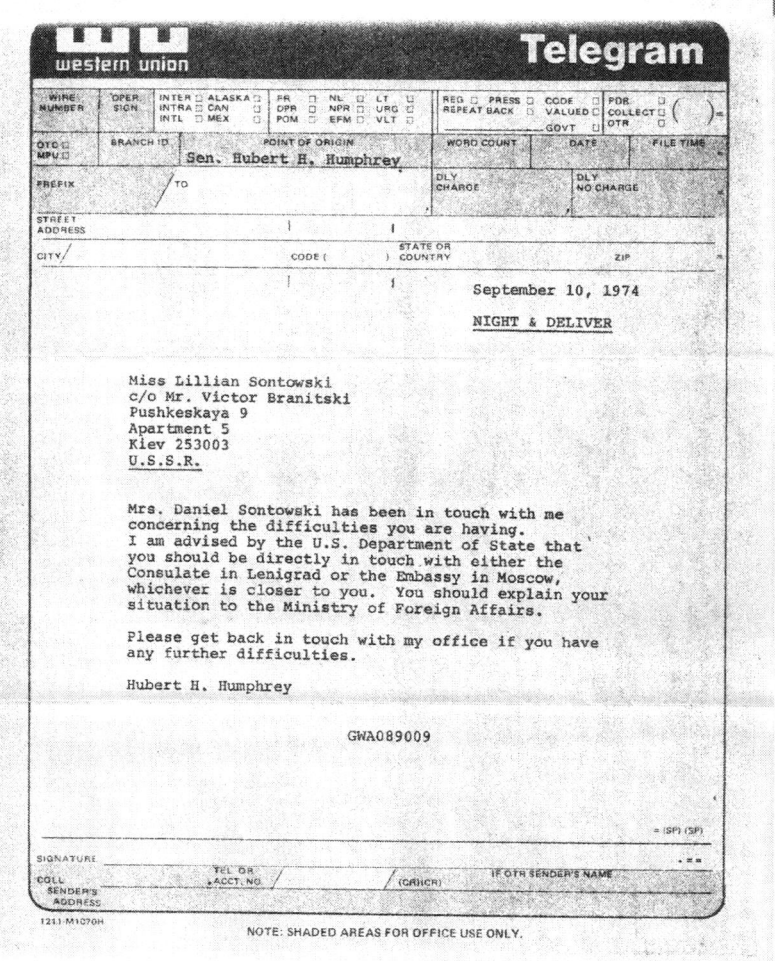

Senator Humphrey's telegram sent to my Kyiv address

Lilli's relatives had gone back to Moldova, there were no friends with flowers. We actually were just expecting to discuss our case with the director to confirm an appointment for the marriage. It was a chilly day, Lilli had a fever, and since she had only packed summer clothes for her trip to the Soviet Union she wore jeans and one of my sweaters. We were accompanied by only my mother and brother who had to wait outside on the street while we went in for our interview. Director Stavitskaya, who kept us waiting for several hours, ordered us into a small office where she sternly lectured us about what "bad" people we were. Then, to our surprise, she gave us the signed Marriage Certificate right then and there!

It was official, we were finally married! Rather than hearing the customary congratulations from the Director she ordered us out of the office saying, "now get out so that my eyes will not see you anymore. OUT!" (*теперь убирайтесь, чтобы мои глаза больше не видели вас, вон!*). She was so vicious and full of malice on our wedding day. My mom remarked "what a lowlife scum, she spoiled so many nerves!" (*вот сволочь, сколько нервов попортила нам, дрянь*)!

No wedding dress, just jeans and a sweater

Our marital bliss did not last long. Three days later on September 13th, 1974 Lilli was kicked out of the country. The three days we spent in Kyiv as husband and wife will always be remembered as a gift from the Lord. During those three days Lilli applied for a temporary residence permit since she was afraid to leave me alone for fear that the Soviets would take me into the army or worse. At the OVIR office (Department of Visas and Registrations) the colonel in charge pressed Lilli to give up her American citizenship in order to stay with me in Kyiv. I firmly told her not to do it. If she gave up her American passport she would not be able to leave the Soviet Union, the same as all Soviet citizens who were prisoners within their own country. Her petition was denied on the spot. I remember her saying to the colonel "why are you torturing me?" She said it in Russian (зачем вы меня мучаете?)

Lilli was flying out of Kyiv to go to Moscow and then via Amsterdam to go home to Minneapolis. In the morning on the way to the airport we were followed by two KGB agents in dark suits. While we were waiting for the flight at Kyiv airport, two more agents sat across from us, covering their faces with a newspaper just like in a spy thriller. The KGB wanted to make sure Lilli was leaving for good. Lilli let them know they weren't fooling anyone when she waved at them and asked them how they were doing. Since we were eating ice cream she even offered to buy them a cone.

That same afternoon we arrived in Moscow for Lilli to catch the Pan American flight home to America. When the plane arrived it was time to say a final goodbye realizing that it could be the last time that we might see each other. Going through customs before boarding the plane Lilli had one more nerve-wracking test. She had hidden her diamond wedding ring on her body. Taking gold or gems out of the Soviet Union was strictly forbidden, warranting arrest. Thankfully, she was able to smuggle it out without notice.

When I returned to Kyiv on the evening flight I learned two days later that I was no longer employed with The Institute of Light Industry as an instructor. I had to find a job, any job, right away so as not to be branded a *"тунеядец,"* a person that is not gainfully employed, a parasite. The motto for the Soviet Union in those days was "if anyone will not work, neither let him eat." I found employment at the local maintenance office, ZHEK, as an odd jobs worker (*разнорабочий*). It should be noted that, back then, if a person was not employed within one month the authorities would evict him from his apartment and send him out of the city to the countryside where there was no shortage of odd jobs. My boss obviously knew my predicament, offering me a job under one condition--I would have to give him my entire monthly salary in order to keep my city residence (*прописка*).

Because of the delay of our marriage, Lilli's return to the U.S. was delayed by several weeks. Consequently, the school year had started so she was placed on sabbatical for that first semester of her teaching position at Robbinsdale and Armstrong High Schools. Thankfully, she did not lose her job. She and her friend Kristi (who, remember, was Lilli's traveling companion when we met), began a letter writing campaign in an effort to have me released from the Soviet Union. Lilli wrote to Minnesota Senators Hubert Humphrey and Walter Mondale asking them for help in our case. Lilli wrote to Senator Henry Jackson from Washington who was the Chairman of the Interior and Insular Affairs Committee as well as to Dr. Henry Kissinger, Secretary of State. There were letters written to the American Embassy in Moscow. Senator Humphrey contacted Russian Ambassador Anatoly Dobrynin in Washington as well as Y. Galishnikov, Director of the Russian Consular Division.

United States Senate
WASHINGTON, D.C. 20510

February 21, 1975

His Excellency
Anatoly F. Dobrynin
Russian Embassy
1125 Sixteenth Street, N.W.
Washington, D. C. 20036

Dear Mr. Ambassador:

Mrs. Lilliana Branitski, 2629 France Avenue,
North, Minneapolis, Minnesota 55422, has been in
touch with me concerning her husband, Victor
Serafimovich Branitski, who applied last September
1974 for an exit visa to the United States. It is
my understanding from Department of State officials
that Mr. Branitski's application still remains
pending and I would like to express my interest in
this case in light of what I feel to be surrounding
compassionate circumstances.

The Branitskis have waited patiently for over
a year to be re-united. They encountered extensive
difficulties in obtaining permission to marry, in
acquiring a marriage license, and then in the actual
marriage ceremony. They were finally married on
September 10, 1974 in Kiev. Mrs. Branitski applied
for a temporary residence visa at the OVIR office in
Kiev but her application was denied. She subsequently
returned to the United States to await the arrival of
her husband.

Any efforts on your part to help expedite a
favorable decision on Mr. Branitski's visa application
will be so very much appreciated. Many thanks.

Sincerely,

Hubert H. Humphrey

Letter from Senator Humphrey to Russian Ambassador
Dobrynin

Waiting For Exit Visa And House Arrest

For the next nine months I impatiently waited to receive my exit visa. I checked with the OVIR office regularly but the answer was always the same--NYET! I had to find some odd jobs in addition to my "money maker" arrangement with ZHEK, to support myself. I sold my keyboard, records, and American jeans Lilli had sent me. Several times unfamiliar girls approached me on the street, striking up a conversation, pretending to know me while someone took candid photos. It was a KGB setup to compromise me. I assumed they would send the photos to Lilli to turn her against me (fortunately she didn't receive any).

I missed Lilli very much and found myself praying to God for help. The thought that I might not see her again was difficult to bear. But somehow the thought that someday we would be together gave me hope and encouragement. If I only knew 2 Peter 1:4 --"He has granted to us His precious and magnificent promises, in order that by them you might become partakers of the divine nature, having escaped the corruption that is in the world."

Finally, on Friday afternoon, April 11th, I was notified by the OVIR office that I was granted the exit visa. I called Mr. Huff at the American Embassy in Moscow to let him know so that I could be issued the American entry visa. He was genuinely glad to hear the good news since he, Consul George Fourier, and Ambassador Walter Stoessel had been fighting for our reunion for the past 9 months. The American visa did not take long to be approved and I was scheduled to leave for the United States May 20th, 1975.

I finally breathed a sigh of relief imagining reuniting soon with my sweetheart wife. I said my final goodbyes to my relatives and friends who believed in us and stood with us to the end. For the last time I wandered the streets of the city where I was born, treasuring the famous Kyiv chestnut trees (the symbol of the city) that were in full bloom that spring. I went for the last time to the beautiful Kyiv beach and swam in the Dnieper river with friends.

They say home is where your heart is. My heart, with definite prompting from the Lord, was with Lilli, my beloved, beautiful, courageous wife who never for a moment gave up praying and fighting for our future together. In Proverbs chapter 31, there is a description of a worthy Godly wife:

"An excellent wife, who can find?" (I, by God's grace, did! Thank you, Lord Jesus)

For her worth is far above jewels.

The heart of her husband trusts in her, (unequivocally)

And he will have no lack of gain.

She does him good and not evil

All the days of her life

Strength and dignity are her clothing,

And she smiles at the future.

She opens her mouth in wisdom (Lilli is extremely smart and organized, she was salutatorian of her high school class and graduated summa cum laude from the University of Minnesota)

And the teaching of kindness is on her tongue.

She looks well to the ways of her household,

And does not eat the bread of idleness.

Her children rise up and bless her (our children and grandchildren simply adore her)

Her husband also, and he praises her (BIG TIME!)

Charm is deceitful and beauty is vain,

But the woman who fears the Lord, she shall be praised…"

My darling Lilli

KGB Evil Plot

With my air ticket purchased, passport and entry visa in hand, and 100 US dollars in my pocket (Soviets were allowed to exchange only $100 dollars worth of rubles when leaving the country) I was packed and ready to leave. My mom called me from her school office Monday afternoon, May 20th, 1974 and asked me to come see her ASAP without telling me anything. I sensed something was wrong. I ran up Pushkinskaya Street where our apartment was to Proreznaya Street (formerly Sverdlova Street) where mom's School #48 was located. It took me less than five minutes. Huffing and puffing I entered her office. Mom was sitting in her chair seemingly distraught. Her face was pale. "Vitya, I just had a conversation with a parent whose son attends our school. She told me that you are not going anywhere tomorrow and that your air tickets are canceled!" What!?

Then my mom told me how the lady's husband, a KGB colonel by the name of Schevchenko, was present at a KGB secret meeting the night before, Sunday, and how it was decided that a "trained military interpreter" (this is me) simply cannot be allowed to emigrate to the United States despite all the efforts from the American side. At that moment I refused to believe my own mother. "Mom, it is impossible, I have an entry visa to America! It is a misunderstanding!" My mom started crying saying that when the colonel's wife told her the story she also said that both she and her husband were shocked at the decision and did not sleep all night. My mom also told me that when the lady talked to her she pleaded with my mother that their conversation remain strictly confidential saying, "if the KGB finds out that I talked to you my husband and our entire family will be ruined. We love and respect you as our school principal and our son thinks so highly of you. My husband and I felt it was our duty to warn you at least." Those were her words.

Since I refused to believe my own mother, my mom pleaded with the lady (when she came to pick up her son after school), asking her to meet with me. She reluctantly agreed. That same evening I went to the designated area that the lady specified for the meeting on Bolshaya Zhitomirskaya Street and waited on the third floor of the old apartment building. It was 9 p.m. I did not realize that she was already there hiding in a dark corner. When she suddenly appeared I was shocked out of my socks. She had on a hat with a veil over her face so that I could not see her features. She was the first to speak, "Victor, everything your mother told you is true. Here is what will be happening: you will be summoned to the KGB Central Building on Korolenko Street tomorrow morning. The interrogator will first try to say pleasant things about you, promising a great career and ultimately persuading you to give up your marriage to your American wife. If you don't agree he will raise his voice, calling you names and will try to provoke you to a physical confrontation. At this point other agents will enter the room, subdue you and put you in a prison cell that is directly beneath his office. Eventually, they will give you an injection of turpentine to eliminate you. I advise you to stay calm and not be provoked by the interrogator's remarks. Other than that I don't know what else to say. I am so sorry."

Those were her last words. She turned around and left crying, asking me to leave 15 minutes later. As I stood there in complete disbelief my first thought was how could they do it to me and my wife knowing that a number of American diplomats were involved; that I was in possession of my entry visa to the US; that I had a telegram from Senator Humphrey's office in Washington; and that Soviet Ambassador Dobrynin was aware of our case. (I did not know at the time that Secretary of State, Dr. Henry Kissinger, was directly involved and presented our case to Russian officials both in Washington and Moscow before signing the Helsinki Declaration on August 2nd 1975). How could the KGB have the nerve to pull this off at the eleventh hour?

Early the next morning there was a knock at our door at Pushkinskaya Street. The mailman served me a summons to appear at the Committee for State Security (Komitet Gosudarstvennoj Bezopasnosti--that is how you get the acronym for KGB). I signed the attached receipt acknowledging receipt of the summons (повестка). It stated in bold letters that in case of failure to appear I would be forcefully brought to the designated facility. Appointment time: 10 a.m. My mom was agitated and said that she was going with me, "I will show those bastards a thing or two!" (Я им, блядям, покажу)!

We walked for about 25 minutes to get to Korolenko 15. I remember it was chilly that morning and I was wearing a sweater that Lilli had given me. Exactly at 10 a.m. I knocked at the indicated office door and walked in. Mom sat on the bench outside the office. There was a guard standing at the door with an AK-47. Need I say it was a little intimidating. The uniformed captain sitting at the table motioned for me to sit down across from him. There was a strong tobacco smell in the office. I was not a smoker and the smell irritated my eyes. I was a little nervous and yet somewhat calm and assured. I was aware of the upcoming scenario and now, in retrospect, realize it was Jesus Who calmed me and helped me to maintain my composure.

KGB building where I was interrogated in 1975

The captain told me that he was familiar with my situation (no kidding). "Victor", he started, "you are the son of a prominent school director and highly decorated colonel, a first lieutenant yourself, talented keyboardist (he said he knew our music group, Sadko), skilled soccer player," and on and on. "Look how many beautiful girls are out there you could be dating. Why an American? Don't we have enough of our own?" (что, своих не хватаем)? "You have such a great career in front of you" (All along I am thinking, what a jerk! I lost my teaching job--KGB doing--and now have to do some manual jobs to make a living. What bright future are you talking about, moron)!? He continued, "divorce her, for your own good, otherwise you will be sorry later on." He was getting nasty at that point and started calling me names.

Now it was my turn to talk. "Comrade Captain, my only offense is that I deeply love my wife whom I've known for four years. She is of the same heritage as I am with Polish-Ukrainian blood. We asked the OVIR office (KGB subsidiary) for permission for her to obtain a temporary residence permit so that she could stay with me in Kyiv but she was denied. Immigration authorities (another KGB subsidiary) kicked her out of the country three days after we were legally married according to Soviet law. Honestly, what would you do if you were me?" I felt as if somebody was speaking through me, giving me the right words to say. I now know WHO it was!

The puzzled captain did not know what to say. He seemed confused and, I would say, embarrassed. The conversation was not going according to his plan. I remained calm and collected (again, it had to be the Lord Who gave me strength and wisdom to reason with the captain). He stood up from his chair and went to an adjacent small room which had a phone on the wall. He dialed a two digit number extension and I heard him whispering, "Comrad lieutenant colonel, I don't know what to do with him." At that moment my mother entered the room, took my hand and we both quietly left. The captain was still on the phone listening to instructions from his superior officer and did not see us leave.

You might ask, how was my mom able to enter the room since there was a guard at the door? Let me explain. There was a long hallway where my mom was sitting. At the end of the hallway was the officers' dining room. Anyone going to the dining room had to pass the office where my mom was sitting. A number of high ranking officers who passed by knew my mom. Recognizing her, they stopped by to say hello, asking what she was doing there and if she needed help. You are wondering how they knew my mother? Well, she was the Director of School #48 for many years. Whenever KGB officers had big meetings they rented my mom's school #48 which had a big hall (актовый зал) for close to 500 people. The KGB did not have a large auditorium at their facility.

Now, the guard does not talk but he has ears. He probably assumed that my mom was someone important. So, when my mom saw through the tiny crack in the door that where there had been two shadowy figures there was now only one (that is when the captain stood and went to call his boss and I remained seated), my mom said to the guard in a commanding voice, "young man, move aside" (а ну-ка, сынок, отойди) and he did! My mom firmly took me by the hand and we slowly walked out of the captain's office and then through the side door to the street.

A taxi with the green light on (which meant it was vacant) came straight at us from nowhere (it was always a problem to catch a taxi cab those days - this one was God sent). Mom flagged him down and we quickly got in. Mom was sitting next to the driver and told me to hide in the back seat, lying flat. When we drove not even 100 yards I saw in the rear view mirror how the captain and the guard ran out onto the street, weapons drawn, their faces bright red. It took us less than five minutes to get home. When I was unlocking our apartment door I heard the phone ringing inside. Mom answered the phone in her usual authoritative voice, "hello, I'm listening." "Comrade Branitskaya, where is your son, Victor?" said the male voice on the other end. "My son is not at home. He went to America to join his wife," mom replied. "Drop the nonsense. Five minutes ago he was in my office" said the Captain. "Please do not cause a conflicting situation. Victor is now under house arrest until further orders!" and he hung up.

For the next ten days I stayed at home under house arrest guarded by two KGB agents who stood outside day and night to prevent me from leaving my apartment. Our apartment on Pushkinskaya Street 9, apartment 5 was on the second floor. The ceiling of my room was painted in the colors and shape of the American flag in Lilli's honor. It was visible from the street. For the benefit of my two "KGB bodyguards" I played the American national anthem on my keyboard or my favorite Chicago song, "Saturday In The Park, I think it was the Fourth of July." Lilli had sent me the Chicago Transit Authority album earlier which was a small musical sensation in Kyiv. People walking on our street would stop to listen to the music. Sometimes a group of people would gather which was not to the liking of my "bodyguards." The Chicago song goes "I think it was the Fourth of July." How I wished then that I would celebrate the Fourth of July with my sweetheart. The Lord Jesus fulfilled the desire of my heart in just a little over a month. I was allowed to leave the Soviet Union on May 31, 1975. My first Fourth of July with my wedded wife in Minneapolis was unforgettable.

In order to make an international phone call one had to go to the main post office station. Since I was under house arrest it was my good friend, Vladimir, who was able to contact Lilli to inform her of the house arrest situation so she could contact the American Embassy with yet another problem that needed to be solved. Think about it, the KGB could have come to our apartment at any time to arrest me and put me in prison rather than keep me under house arrest. The only plausible explanation I can think of is that the Embassy was involved and the Soviets wanted to avoid unnecessary publicity. The genie was out of the bottle, so to say, and they realized they had lost the battle. The Lord Jesus pulled me through that last hurdle. To Him alone be the glory!

Leaving Kyiv To Join Lilli In America

I left Kyiv May 31st, 1975. My mother and brother, Vadim, flew with me to Moscow where I boarded the flight to New York. My mom fainted at the Vnukovo Moscow airport as we said our final goodbyes. Lots of tears were shed with assurances to write to each other. I looked at my family for the last time, not sure if I would ever see them again. After I left for America my family in Kyiv suffered the consequences. My mother was ousted from her position as Director of School #48. She was under an enormous amount of stress, resulting in a serious illness. My brother, Vadim, who was Senior Sound Engineer of Ukranian Television with over fifty employees under his supervision was demoted and, eventually, kicked out of his job. His wife, Lirena, a ballerina who had travelled the world with the Bolshoi Ballet also lost her job.

I boarded the plane, Pan American Airlines, sat by the window and closed my eyes. The thought that I would soon be reunited with my sweetheart Lilli cheered me up. The flight attendant came up to ask me if I was OK. She was so nice and smiling (what a drastic change from the stern looks and unfriendliness of the Aeroflot flight attendants on the Kyiv -Moscow flight). She also asked what was my final destination. I told her about Lilli and she congratulated me, wishing me many happy years with my wife. "Welcome to America!" she said cheerfully. I needed that. It was like an entirely different world for me. People were friendly! Another flight attendant came up to me, smiling, and offered me a soft drink. She already knew my story and wished me well. The plane smelled nice unlike my previous flight and ALL other Aeroflot flights I had previously experienced. The flight was surprisingly smooth. I came to the conclusion that Soviet Aeroflot passenger planes were suited for cargo delivery not for people. Delicious food was served and then we even watched a movie. This is sheer paradise I thought and took a small nap.

America!
    When we were approaching New York looking out of my window I could see the Statue of Liberty, the beautiful sky-scrapers, ocean harbors. It seemed like the whole city was sparkling in the sun welcoming me. What a sight!

    When we landed the captain announced on the intercom that I should stay in my seat until everyone left the plane. I was somewhat nervous. When the last passenger exited, two gentlemen dressed in suits came up to me. With a broad smile one of them said, "Mr. Branitski, we are from the F.B.I. It is like the KGB in your country but we are much friendlier people--welcome to the U.S." His welcome was followed by a firm handshake. I was instantly relieved. The two agents escorted me to the immigration authorities. After spending some time answering questions and filling out immigration forms in a special room I was escorted to the gate where Lilli was nervously waiting. "When I saw all the passengers exiting from your plane except for you I started worrying! " she said.

She looked terrific in her Ukrainian outfit I had sent her a while ago, Our hugs and kisses were coupled with tears of joy. King David writes in Psalm 37:4 "Delight yourself in the Lord, and He will give you the desires of your heart." The Lord certainly answered Lilli's many prayers and gave her the desire of her heart. Even though I was not a born again Christian at that time I sensed deep down in my heart that God had performed a miracle and reunited me with my sweetheart.

We took a taxi into New York City. It was in the taxi that I whispered to Lilli that I had a surprise for her. I had a loose Siberian diamond stuck to my back molar with a piece of chewing gum. See, she was not the only diamond smuggler in the family. In New York we stayed at the Abbey Victoria hotel which was on 7th Ave and 51st Street. For three days Lilli delighted in showing me the wonders of this magnificent city of 8.5 million people. I arrived with only the clothes on my back and a suitcase full of Ukrainian souvenirs. I enjoyed a shopping trip at the iconic New York Macy's store. We even took in a Broadway show starring Bette Midler.

First days in America
Rockefeller Center New York City

After staying in New York we flew to Washington D.C. where a friend from Kyiv, Olga, was waiting for us with her newly acquired American friend Slavko. Lilli and I went to the Senate Building where we met Senator Walter Mondale who was a Junior Senator from Minnesota at the time and whose office was very helpful in facilitating our case. Senator Mondale was very interested in talking with us as we thanked him for his assistance. We also went to see Senator Hubert Humphrey who, unfortunately, was not in his office at the time. We thanked his staff who did so much for us. They were glad to know that the telegram I had received from the Senator was instrumental in assisting in our struggle with Soviet authorities. Both Senator Hubert Humphrey and Senator Mondale from Minnesota served the United States as Vice-Presidents.

From Washington DC we flew to Minneapolis saying goodbye to our friends. Yaroslav Billy was the first Ukrainian American to greet me in the U.S. Later he moved to Minneapolis where he married his beautiful wife Oksana. We have been friends for 45 years and I had the privilege of leading Slavko to the Lord when I became a Christian. Even though Yaroslav Billy was an electrical engineer by profession he was also an incredible Ukrainian folk dancer. He performed with the New Jersey Ballet Company, Metropolitan Ballet, International Dance Ensemble of New York and Ukrainian Dance Company of Minnesota.

INTERNATIONAL DANCE ENSEMBLE U.S.A.   DIRECTION WADIM SULIMA

Slavko Billy with his signature Ukrainian Hopak jump

At the Minneapolis airport we were warmly greeted by Lilli's family and friends. Her parents, Daniel and Sonia, gave us an apartment in their fourplex house in Robbinsdale that Daniel had built himself. While building the house, Daniel enlisted the help of his sons, George and Eddie, with the purpose of training them in the art of building and craftsmanship. George often recalls how hard he worked with his dad on the house. "While my friends would enjoy playing football and baseball I had to help my dad on weekends to build the American dream." All the Sontowski boys inherited an incredible work ethic and European craftsmanship skills from their father, a master carpenter. All three of them, Danny Jr. included, are highly skilled builders and designers who had their own successful construction company (they built our beautiful house in Maple Grove).

Our American Wedding

Lilli wanted to have a proper Christian wedding ceremony to celebrate our marriage. Our American church wedding was set for July 19th, 1975. (So, we celebrate two wedding dates, Ukrainian wedding September 10th, 1974 and American wedding July 19th, 1975). July 19th was a memorable day in my life. We had a lovely wedding ceremony with beautiful flowers (Lilli worked at Hogland's flower shop in Robbinsdale part time and the owner, Frank Neu, made fabulous arrangements for our special day). The photographer took beautiful pictures of the family and bridal party (Kristi whom I met with Lilli in Kyiv in 1970 was the maid of honor). Pastor Frank Wloch from the Polish Baptist Church came all the way from Chicago to marry us. I remember when he asked Lilli if she promised to "love her husband till death do us part", he asked her to repeat after him "I promise" in Ukrainian "обіцяю" (she had been expecting the vows to be in Russian). Until this very day I remind her of her promise in Ukrainian and get a broad smile from her in return. My angel, we are still pretty much in love, right, honey? In Proverbs 12:4 we read "An excellent wife is the crown of her husband." Once in a while I ask my sweetheart if she is my CROWN. She approvingly nods in return.

American church wedding, July 19, 1975

Kristi was our maid of honor

Lilli's parents

Chapter 6   LILLI'S STORY

My heritage is Polish on my father's side and Ukrainian on my mother's side. I grew up in a home where Polish, Ukrainian and Russian were spoken. My brothers, George, Edward, and Daniel Jr. and I were brought up in a Christian home, going to American Sunday school every Sunday morning and to Russian Baptist Church every Sunday afternoon. My father, Daniel, was a deacon in the church. My mother, Sonia, sang in the church choir. I was actually the church pianist from an early age (five years old) because no one else knew how to play the piano. In fact, as a young girl I learned to read Russian while playing the church hymns over and over again during choir practice.

My brothers and I developed a great work ethic, following the example of our parents. Daniel was a master carpenter who could do just about anything. He drew up the plans and built a large house for the family from the ground up. He was a master craftsman specializing in beautiful wood work. All his children and grandchildren are proud owners of beautifully crafted furniture--china cabinets, grandfather clocks, hope chests, tables, etc. He and Sonia were incredible gardeners. Sonia always had a beautiful flower garden and worked in the huge vegetable garden together with Daniel. The family was eating delicious organic vegetables well before it was the "in thing."

European Adventure

When I was a freshman at the University of Minnesota, my best friend Kristi and I embarked on a three month trip to Europe. With the aid of Arthur Frommer's book, "Europe on Five Dollars a Day" we traveled all around Europe to 13 different countries The adventures included exploration of Kristi's Norwegian heritage and culminated in a trip to Eastern Europe, visiting Poland, Russia, and Ukraine. The trip to Ukraine had been arranged in such a way to connect with my relatives with whom there had been almost no contact since the beginning of World War II.

Sonia's Story

Sonia Pronko was born in the village Chumaki, Piatihatki region in the central part of Ukraine in the vicinity of Dnepropetrovsk. When she was a young girl the Nazis were going into Ukrainian villages, rounding up all the young people and transporting them by cattle car to Germany to use them for forced labor in factories, forests, and farms. Sonia was 19 years old when the Germans came to her village in 1943. She was separated from her mother and younger sister and forced to go to Germany. (Sonia's father, Stepan, had been drafted into the Red Army. He died in 1941 when the Nazis invaded Ukraine). Rather than working in a factory, Sonia was one of the luckier ones who was sent to work on a farm. Thankfully, the family that took her did not treat her badly. They were decent people and were not harsh with her. She had to wake up early to milk the cows and was busy all day with chores on the farm. It was when the war ended that she was placed in a Displaced Persons camp in Germany. That is where she met her future husband.

Sonia Sontowski (1924-2009)

Daniel's Story

Daniel Sontowski was of Polish descent, but born in Tomsk, Siberia in 1910. How did his family end up in Siberia you ask? In the second half of the 19th century there was a voluntary migration of Polish families to Siberia in search of a better life. People were promised free land and building materials in an effort to colonize uninhabited Russian territories. Because of the economic crisis in Poland, Daniel's father, Frederic, moved his family and 200 other families from Poland to the Krasnoyarsk region of Siberia to claim free land.

3,000 mile trek from Siberia back to Poland

At first it was very difficult to adjust to the climate, the harsh winters. The families worked to clear the forest where no one had ever set foot before. Little by little they cleared the land and had a good harvest. By 1912 the Sontowski family had 200 hectares of land, 60 horses, and 40 cows. Frederic was a lawyer, he was the leader of the colony. He was loved and respected by the entire community. The colony preserved the Polish language, traditions, and farming methods. At the local primary school, children were learning Russian as a foreign language.

In 1917 the October Revolution began. The Bolsheviks confiscated crops, cattle, horses,--everything. Frederic was killed during this time. His wife, Carolina, and other Poles packed up their children to try to get back to Poland. Daniel was ten years old when they made this 3,000 mile trek across Siberia to return to Poland. Daniel recalled walking barefoot, at times, across the cold ground.

The family settled in Hotin which was in western Ukraine, but was given to Poland by Lenin. Again they had to clear the fields and start anew. As the boys grew (Alexander, Ivan, Paul, and Daniel) they were able to help Carolina work the land.

Daniel was married in 1936 to Helena Kundeus. He was very hard-working and well known as having the best farm and orchard in the region. He was always willing and happy to help his friends and neighbors. In 1939 Daniel was taken straight from the field (without even a chance to say goodbye to his family) to fight in the Polish army against Germany. Daniel was captured by the Germans and sent to hard labor in a German prison camp

In 1941 the Ukrainian Banderivtsi killed Daniel's wife and toddler son. This organization of Ukrainian nationalists was engaged in various atrocities, including murder of civilians, whom were mostly ethnic Poles. The Ukrainian death squads carried out massacres, targeting Polish villagers and other minorities. Helena was buried alive in a ditch. In 1942 a friend from Daniel's village was captured and sent to the same prison. He had to tell Daniel what had happened to his family.

While in prison, Daniel was mistreated and nearly died several times. But he found a way to stay alive. Because of his incredible craftsmanship skills he could build furniture as ordered by the camp Komandant. The Komandant kept Daniel alive so as to have more furniture crafted for his wife.

When the war ended Daniel was placed in a Displaced Person's camp where he met Sonia. They were married in 1946. After some years of being transferred from place to place in the American zone in Germany, Daniel and Sonia were granted entry to the United States. In 1949 they traversed the ocean by ship with many other immigrants who were excited to arrive at Ellis Island, seeing the Statue of Liberty for the first time.

Sonia with Daniel (1910-1991)

Daniel and Sonia married in Germany 1946

My parents lived in Brooklyn for two years before moving to Buffalo, New York where I was born in 1951

When in New York, with the aid of the Red Cross, Sonia was able to get in contact with her family in Ukraine by letter. They had had no contact since the war. They were able to correspond with each other but, because of the Cold War, had no hope of ever seeing each other.

Connecting With Relatives In Poland And Ukraine

While Kristi and I were on our European adventure we visited my cousin Paulina (my father's niece) in Poland. I remember being amazed at how much she looked like my father (but much shorter). They lived on a farm and asked me to relate to my father how great their life now was compared to what it had been years ago. I cried just about the entire time I was with them because it was so upsetting to see that they were actually very poor, living in a small house with a single light bulb dangling from the ceiling.

Daniel's niece Paulina in Poland

I also met my cousin Volodia and his daughter Marusia who came to Kyiv from the Dubno/Rovno region of Ukraine. This is where Daniel had his homestead but it was no longer Poland, it was now Ukraine. It was while visiting these relatives that I heard the tragic story of my father's first family. My parents never wanted to talk about the war. They did not tell us anything about the struggles they had endured during the war years. They did talk about it with their friends, though. My brothers and I later heard more stories from these friends than we ever heard from our own parents.

Daniel's nephew, Volodia and Marusia

The main purpose of my trip to Ukraine in 1970 was to connect with Sonia's sister Tonia and Sonia's mother Efrosiniya. My mother had been separated from her family for 30 years. It was wonderful to meet my grandmother and aunt in Kishinev, Moldova.

Grandma Efrosinia and Aunt Tonia

When I returned home to America I encouraged my mom to take the bold step, to travel to Ukraine and Moldova to see her family. Sonia was afraid because after World War II all Soviet citizens were required to return to their homeland. But it was rumored in the German camps that those who returned to the Soviet Union usually ended up with a death sentence in Siberia. This, in actuality, was true. The Soviets did not want any eyewitness accounts about how much better life was in Europe than in the closed society of the Soviet Union. Daniel convinced Sonia to assume a new identity as a Polish citizen so as not to return to the Soviet Union. He gave her the identity of his deceased wife, Helena Kundeus.

All those years Sonia thought there was no chance to ever see her family again. BUT, in 1971 I convinced her to make the trip. After a 30 year separation there certainly was a very joyful reunion in Kishinev!

Sonia's sister and mother

91

Meeting the Love of my Life

It was during this trip to Ukraine in 1970 that I met the very handsome and charming Victor Branitski in Kyiv. He swept me off my feet, he melted my heart. I guess it was love at first sight. We did carry on a very long distance love correspondence via the mail. But, being realistic, I knew it was an impossible love--hence the letter to Victor that it was a FUTILE situation. I spent the summer of 1972 working in Germany with the specific plan in mind to end the summer with a trip to Kyiv to say goodbye to Victor. But, we realized our love was strong and we were willing to fight for it. It was not until two years later that we were actually able to marry in Kyiv (as previously described by Victor).

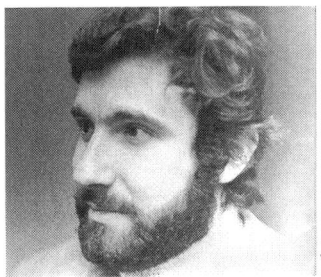
Victor, my love!

After overcoming the obstacles we faced in the Soviet Union we have been blessed with a wonderful life in America. We were able to eventually bring Victor's mother and brother and family to Minnesota.

We have celebrated 46 wonderful years of marriage. The Lord has blessed us with four beautiful children and 7 wonderful grandchildren. They are the joy of our life.

Our 15th anniversary

Our family, our joy!

My brothers, Edward, George, Daniel Sontowski Jr.

Our children, Tania, Anthony, Michael, Andrei

Chapter 7   BEGINNING A NEW LIFE IN JESUS

Coming To Christ

When I was teaching at the University of Minnesota several students in my first year Russian class were Christians. I remember how they were asking me about the condition of the church in the USSR. I told them about visiting the Baptist Church in Kyiv with my future mother-in-law, Sonia, in 1971, and how impressed I was to hear the Pastor preaching from the history filled Gospel of Luke. I also told them that Christians in the USSR were persecuted for their faith in Christ and a number of them were exiled to Siberia for their convictions, their children taken away and placed in state run orphanages to be "reprogrammed."

One of my students asked me to translate a Christian tract into Russian which I did. The text was crystal clear: Jesus Christ, the historic figure of Christianity, died for our sins on the cross of Calvary and rose again on the third day so "that whoever believes in Him should not perish, but have eternal life." The tract also stated that "the Son of God has come, and has given us understanding, in order that we might know Him who is true, and we are in Him who is true, in His Son Jesus Christ. This is the true God and eternal life" 1 John 5:20.

That same student asked me to also translate a pamphlet that, essentially, was a Bible study showing how Old Testament prophecies were fulfilled in the New Testament. As I was working on the translation, digging deeper into Bible verses I became convinced that the Bible was truly the Word of God.

I realized for the first time that "whoever" in John 3:16 could be ME! And that Jesus Christ is God incarnate Who gives us understanding so that we might know Him.

When our first child, beautiful Tania, was born I remembered the Bible passage from Matthew where Jesus said "Truly I say to you, unless you are converted and become like children, you shall not enter the kingdom of heaven" Matthew 18:3. As I looked at Tania and saw how she would love me as her father I could understand how we need to come to our Heavenly Father through His Son Jesus with a sincere, childlike faith based upon His promises.

After looking back at my life, I no longer questioned the existence of God. Looking at the wasted 30 years of my life, I realized that I had broken God's laws many times and I needed Him to forgive me for those sins. I knew that forgiveness was possible only through Jesus Christ and Him alone. It is a gift of God. Becoming a father is also a gift of the Lord. "Behold, children are a gift of the Lord" Psalm 127:3.

I knew that I could not earn or deserve my salvation by good works. Brother Gene Jankowski, who was my witness at my water baptism, taught me Ephesians 2:8,9 which says that "For by GRACE you have been saved through FAITH; and that not of yourselves, it is the GIFT of GOD; not as a result of works, that no one should boast".

I remember my student, Nick, witnessing to me quoting Romans 3:23, "For all have sinned and fall short of the glory of God" (I agreed that I was a sinner) and then three Chapters later, in Romans 6:23, he quoted "For the wages of sin is death" then he stopped... Just think about it, you acknowledge that you are a sinner and realize that the wages of your sin is death, separation from God and eternal punishment in hell, enough grounds to be scared, don't you agree? Then Nick said "I have Good News for you!" I remember telling him "roll it by me quick!" The second part of the verse is "but the free gift of God is eternal life in Christ Jesus our Lord."

All I needed to do was to REPENT of my sins and RECEIVE the free Gift of God.   "But as many as RECEIVED Him, (Jesus) to them He gave the right to become children of God, even to those who believe in His name" John 1:12.

Sunday,   May 21st, 1978 was my spiritual birthday. Pastor Frank Wloch came to Minneapolis for an outreach unbeknownst to the fact that Victor, whom he married earlier, was ready to publicly confess Jesus as his Lord and Savior. The Scripture says "that if you confess with your mouth Jesus as Lord, and believe in your heart that God raised Him from the dead, you shall be saved. For with the heart man believes, resulting in righteousness,   and   with   the   mouth   he   confesses, resulting in salvation" Romans 10:9,10.

Jesus told Nicodemus, who was a Pharisee and "a ruler of the Jews," that "unless one is born again, he cannot see the kingdom of God." The Gospel of John, Chapter 3, discribes a fascinating dialogue between Jesus, the Son of God, and Nicodemus, a very religious man, who was not a child of God. It must have been quite a shocker for Nicodemus to learn that his Pharisaic religion was not enough for salvation! It never is. He addressed Jesus as "Rabbi" and "teacher from God," but Jesus knew that Nicodemus needed MORE than a teacher and Rabbi - he needed a SAVIOR. He needed more than RELIGION; he needed complete regeneration of his soul.

Contrasting the two births Jesus pointed out "That which is born of the flesh is flesh (unable to ever change, this is our old sinful nature under the sentence of death) and that which is born of the Spirit is spirit (produces a righteous divine nature incapable of sinning)" John 3:6. Believing in Jesus and receiving Him in your heart makes you a born again believer.

What a glorious day that Sunday, May 21st, was!

I told my father-in-law, Daniel, early in the morning that I want to confess Jesus publicly and be baptized. I had been attending church regularly and voraciously reading the Scripture, I was ready. He was so excited calling several people and asking the deacon of Elim Baptist Church to fill the baptistry with water.

In the Gospel of Mark it says "He who has believed and has been baptized shall be saved but he who has disbelieved shall be condemned" Mark 16:16. Before full immersion in the water ("after being baptized, Jesus went up immediately FROM THE WATER.." Matthew 3:16) Pastor asked me if I believed that Jesus is the Son of God, and also if I believed that God the Father raised Him from the dead. I replied "I believe." Then he said "Upon confession of your faith I baptize you in the name of the Father, and of the Son and of the Holy Spirit. Amen." When I came out of the water and the Pastor was holding my hand, I felt as if I was weightless. I thought at that moment that if he would let go of my hand I would go up like a balloon. I was so thankful that the pastor was firmly holding my hand, I never experienced that feeling before. I started praising the Lord and told the congregation that "someday we, dear brothers and sisters, who believe, will be walking on the golden street like a transparent glass of the New Jerusalem " Revelation 21:21.

The Lord Jesus started taking control of my life almost immediately. The next day, on Monday, I told my Russian language students at the University what happened to me Sunday morning and what a blessing it was to know the Risen Savior Jesus. They told me later that my face was radiating while I was telling them about my born again experience. Apostle Paul wrote to believers in Corinth "Therefore, if any man is in Christ, he is a new creation ("poema" in Greek); the old things passed away; behold, NEW THINGS have come. Now all these things are from God, Who reconciled us to Himself through Christ, and gave us the ministry of reconciliation" 2 Corinthians 5:17,18.

It was as if the Lord turned on His light within me and wanted me to share it with others. Those who are reading these words and know me personally can attest to the fact that I share my faith in Jesus wherever I go. One of the gifts He bestowed on me is the gift of evangelism for which I am so thankful.

Chapter 8 LIFE AND WORK IN THE U.S.

Thanks to Lilli's good family friend, Ursula, Lilli and I landed a job with Control Data Corporation which was one of the most respected computer companies in the U.S. Ursula was the executive secretary to CDC's Vice-President Robert Schmidt. She was a Christian and prayed for us during our marriage saga. We were translating various technical manuals from English to Russian and vice versa. We were a perfect team. Lilli translated from Russian into English, I edited her work. I translated from English to Russian and she was my editor. At that time there were no Russian immigrants in Minneapolis so we really cornered the market. Lilli and I were busy with written translation work for many years.

I was hired as an interpreter for the company. It was fascinating for me to learn about the American computer business. In 1975 CDC came up with the STAR-100, the most powerful and fastest computer. It was placed into service in a Control Data service facility which was considered the first supercomputer in a data center. Later on, the CDC Cyber computer became CDC's main product line and I had the opportunity to interpret for a number of Russian computer specialist delegations that were in awe to observe the Cyber 200/205 in action.

I remember a Russian group of computer engineers who came to Control Data in July of 1978 headed by the famous Soviet economist, Academician Fedorenko. After visiting CDC Headquarters in Bloomington, Minnesota, we went to San Francisco, accompanied by Control Data specialists. At a dinner at Fisherman's Wharf Mr. Fedorenko was asked by the waiter what he would like to drink-- "perhaps Russian vodka?" Fedorenko looked at me grinning,

"Victor, tell this jokester that I am already tired of it in Moscow." Instead he ordered "a true icon" as he put it, Johnnie Walker Black Label Scotch Whisky. The waiter was surprised to hear Fedorenko order the whisky "in a water glass, no ice please!" As the waiter brought the glass of whisky to the table, my American colleagues asked me "will he be OK or will we be losing him soon?" Well, I should mention that the Academician was about 6'2", 300 pounds. He took a liking to the famous San Francisco sourdough bread which he ate with lots and lots of butter. "After that,",he explained, "you can drink all you want since butter does not allow alcohol to penetrate the bloodstream that quickly." So, that was his technique!

When it was time to order dinner the waiter announced "today's specials." Academician ordered three entrees--New York steak, sea bass, and shrimp with, you guessed it, another glass of whisky (same amount). He later belted out "Moscow Nights" LOUDLY as the adjacent tables cheered him on. You'd be surprised to know that after consuming that incredible amount of alcohol (I forgot to mention the several bottles of Californian Russian Valley wine that was consumed), Fedorenko continued to maintain fairly decent conversation offering toasts "for friendship and cooperation" (за дружбу и сотрудничество). The Control Data computer specialist sitting next to me asked, "Victor, aren't you glad you immigrated to the US?"

The next morning at breakfast in our hotel the Russian delegation asked for pickle juice (рассол). "This is how we cure hangovers," they explained. The waiter brought several jars of pickles as the Russians applauded and shouted HOORAY drinking pickle juice. It was on this trip that I talked to Nikolai Fedorenko about my newly found faith in Jesus (I came to the saving knowledge of Jesus Christ May 21, 1978. I will tell you about it later). Fedorenko was born in Ukraine and was glad to know I was Ukrainian. Even though our official conversations were in Russian, he was very happy to have the opportunity to speak Ukrainian with me. The Lord gave me liking in his eyes and he listened with interest as I shared my testimony.

"Victor, you say God is a loving God. Explain to me how is it that when Sodom and Gomorrah were destroyed with brimstone and fire from the Lord out of heaven for their sin of homosexuality, there must have been young children there also. I understand the adults deserve it, but why kids? Aren't they innocent?" I explained that the loving God is also a just God "Who punishes the world for its evil" Isaiah 13:11. When the two angels came to Sodom in Chapter 19 in Genesis, the righteous Lot tried to protect them from the men of the city who surrounded his house and asked for the two men to be given to them "that we may have relations with them." The text says that "the men of Sodom surrounded the house, both young and old, all the people from every quarter" verse 4. When the two angels of God struck the men who were at Lot's doorway with blindness, they struck "both small and great" verse 11.

I explained to Fedorenko that the Bible states that the entire population of Sodom and Gomorrah, kids and adults included, were practicing homosexuality which is evil in the eyes of the Lord. The proof is in the preceding Chapter 18. "And the Lord said, The outcry of Sodom and Gomorrah is indeed great, and their sin is exceedingly grave" verse 20.
Surprisingly, Fedorenko agreed and asked me to tell him more stories from the Scripture. Paul told the church in Rome that "faith comes from hearing, and hearing by the word of Christ" Romans 10:17. I wonder if Nikolai made the most important decision in his life --making peace with Jesus.

University of Minnesota

When Lilli wanted to show me her Alma Mater to introduce me to her former professors at the Department of Slavic Languages I gladly agreed. The Department Chair, Professor Adele Donchenko, offered me a job as a Russian language instructor for which I was so thankful. I absolutely loved teaching at the University of Minnesota. I really enjoyed the students and I would say the feeling was mutual. Three years in a row I was nominated for the Distinguished Teacher's Award. We staged several sketches in Russian and had picnics together which was a lot of fun. I also played soccer for the University Men's Team. I taught for five years at the U of M from 1975 to 1980 and thoroughly enjoyed it.

Carleton College in Northfield

In 1980 I was invited to teach at the prestigious Carleton College. By that time we had two small children Tania (3 years old) and Andrei (one year old). We rented Professor Nau's house on Fourth Street in Northfield while he was out of the country on sabbatical. The campus was beautiful. I was in charge of teaching two Russian classes of very smart Carletonias. The Russian Department Chairman, Professor Joe Shepherd, was very accommodating and hospitable, and we fast became good friends. He was an excellent scholar and a great tennis player among other things. I enjoyed playing tennis with him on warm fall afternoons, obviously losing every time. I remember him and his wife inviting all of us to their house for dinner. It was a special blessing for us especially in the winter time. Their quaint house was always warm and inviting.

The house we lived in was old and poorly insulated. The old wooden floors would creek every time we'd step on it. We would gather the kids on the main floor where the old fireplace was and dress them in double layers. No matter how high we cranked up the heat, we were constantly freezing! I often slept with two sets of pajamas on.

We would play Evie's albums and sing our favorite "Come on, ring those bells, light the Christmas tree, Jesus is the King, born for you and me." And at the end "Jesus, we remember this Your Birthday!". The Lord cheered us up and we felt His invisible presence in our lives.

While at Carleton I attended men's and women's soccer practices and games. As a former player and coach I enjoyed participating in pick-up games offering tips to the players. In 1981 Carleton obtained varsity sport status. The Physical Education department hired me to coach the Carleton Women's Soccer Team. As the season progressed it was very rewarding to see the team improve their skills.

I would be remiss not to mention that an added attraction for us in Northfield was the fact that our friend, Kristi, and her husband, Mark, were living there. Both of them were working in this college town. Kristi was a librarian at Carleton College. Mark was an English literature professor at Saint Olaf College. We enjoy and cherish our friendship with them until this very day. Yes, this is the same Kristi who was traveling with Lilli when we met in Kyiv back in 1970. This year marks fifty years since we have known each other.

IDS - Investors Diversified Services

In the spring of 1982 a friend of Lilli's, Leanne, suggested that I talk to her husband, Dave Laurian, a successful financial planner with IDS, regarding starting a new job in the financial industry. I met Dave, who was a Christian, to discuss the possibility of becoming a financial planner. It was getting harder for me to support our growing family financially. By that time we had Tania, Andrei and Anthony (Michael was born in 1984). My annual income teaching at Carleton was $12,700. Dave told me that I had the ambition and personality to succeed in the financial services industry and encouraged me to consider a career move. We prayed about it and left it in the Lord's hands. It was not an easy decision and it involved much soul searching. Lilli was very supportive and I finally agreed. IDS sent me to their Security School in Chaska, Minnesota where I studied to become a financial planner. I failed my first NASD (National Association of Securities Dealers) exam miserably. It simply was overwhelming for me. Dave encouraged me to press on.

I was assigned to Max Roth's District in Minneapolis and he and IDS Divisional Manager, Tom Turner, whose Division was number one in the country, believed in me and encouraged me to press on to study and pass the needed exam. I will always be grateful to them for their great support and prayers. Meanwhile it was more schooling, more studying of the mysterious world of finances, more weeks away from the family and the second attempt. I failed again, but this time I was close. I scored 64, only six points away from a passing grade. I remember shooting my prayers up to the Lord and asking Him to show me if what I was doing was His will for me and my family. I sincerely asked Him if I were a "Good Steward of my money and time" as I was gearing up toward my third and final attempt. Hooray, I scored 78!

Tom Turner was the first to tell me that I had passed. He was beaming, giving me a big hug. "Victorolla, bubba, (Tom was from Lubbock, Texas), Jesus answered our prayers. Hallelujah!" Max was standing next to him giving me a bear hug (Max Roth was a safety and punter for the Dallas Cowboys shortly after he immigrated to the US. He hails from Germany).

At IDS Top Producers Conference with Max and Kathy Roth

Thus began my career as a financial planner with IDS/American Express. The Lord's blessings accompanied me along the way allowing me to excel and set a national record for productivity in the first eight weeks on the job. As a member of the President's Executive Council, being one of the top producers in the country, I had the privilege of attending company sponsored events around the US and sharing my faith with other financial planners and home office employees. The Lord Jesus gave me that status to attract people to Himself. I was actually an evangelist disguised as a financial planner.

Dave and I led a Bible Study at our office during the lunch break, encouraging financial planners to consider Biblical claims. We explained how a person can obtain salvation by the grace of God through the saving faith in Jesus and HAVE AN ASSURANCE OF IT! "These things I have written to you who believe in the name of the Son of God, in order that you MAY KNOW THAT YOU HAVE ETERNAL LIFE" 1 John 5:13. We also acknowledged that another important precept in the Bible is the teaching of being "a good steward of your money and time." After all, we were entrusted with people's hard earned money and they expected nothing less than our knowledgeable stewardship of their finances. God spoke through prophet Isaiah "Thus says the Lord, your Redeemer, the Holy One of Israel; "I am the Lord your God, Who TEACHES YOU TO PROFIT, Who leads you in a way you should go" Isaiah 48:17.

More planners started attending our Bible Study. Many of my colleagues found that it was helping them grow spiritually as well as professionally. The key verses from Colossians 3:23,24 helped us realize that even though we, de facto, worked for IDS/American Express, in actuality we worked as if for the Lord Jesus in the marketplace, serving Him with our time and treasure. Here is what Apostle Paul writes to the church at Colossae, "Whatever you do, do your work heartily, AS FOR THE LORD rather than for men; knowing that FROM THE LORD you will receive the reward of the inheritance. IT IS THE LORD CHRIST WHOM YOU SERVE" Colossians 3:23,24.

In the fall of 1987 the Vice-President of Operations of IDS/AMERICAN EXPRESS, Mr. Dan Hadaway, contacted me and told me that "the higher management" did not approve of our Bible Study. (In 1984 American Express Company from New York acquired IDS for $780 million). "It is controversial," he said. I tried to explain that we do it during our lunch time (45 min.) bringing our brown bags to the dining room. I also told him about the positive results that we observed with financial planners' work ethics and their increased productivity due to taking to heart the Lord's teaching. I invited him and "the higher management" to observe our growing fellowship and see for themselves the enthusiasm in the group. He politely declined. "What if we move downstairs to the public cafeteria?" I asked. "I am afraid it won't work either," he said. It certainly put a damper on our sincere efforts. I informed our Bible Study group about the company's decision and we all prayed to continue to be faithful to the Lord Jesus despite the overzealous secular New Yorkers.

Apostle Paul admonished Corinthians to "Test yourselves to see if you are in the faith; examine yourselves!" 2 Corinthians 13:5. Well I came home and told Lilli about my conversation. "What are you going to do?" she asked. Please understand that after working for almost five years for the company I accumulated a fair amount of American Express stock through various awards and promotions. I was a couple months away from being fully vested. Lilli's brothers, Sontowski Enterprises, were finishing building a sizable house for our growing family of four children in Maple Grove. Should I wait several months until I am fully vested and then quit or should I quit now?

We prayed for the Lord's leading. It was a difficult decision to make, having been the sole provider for the family with small children, however, the other option was to compromise. The meaning of the word compromise is agreement by concession. The Bible discourages a believer to compromise his convictions. In the Proverbs of Solomon we read, "My son, if sinners entice you do not consent...do not walk in the way with them, keep your feet from their path... He (the Lord) is a shield to those who walk in integrity... discretion will guard you, understanding will watch over you... trust in the Lord with all your heart, and do not lean on your own understanding, in all your ways acknowledge Him, and

He will make your paths straight" Proverbs 1:10,15. 2:7,11. 3:5,6. Apostle Paul encouraged Corinthians not to compromise their faith in Christ with unbelievers, "what has a believer in common with an unbeliever...come out of their midst and be separate, says the Lord" 2 Corinthians 6:15,17.

I wrote a letter of resignation, trusting Jesus for the outcome. At approximately the same time IDS/AMERICAN EXPRESS was downsizing the Divisional Manager positions, letting go of seasoned successful managers and substituting them for younger ones, primarily from the East Coast, with the set salary of $174,000. A class action law suit based on age discrimination ensued. Tom Turner asked me to be a witness as a Bible Study leader who was denied the opportunity to conduct studies, as he put it, "based on the grounds of religious discrimination." I was asked by Tom not to sue the company which I did not plan to do anyways. I was simply called upon to describe religious intolerance that overtly took place in the company.

When I was testifying before the company's hired attorneys I was accompanied by my attorney and good friend Dave S. I briefly shared my testimony about how I came to Christ having formerly been raised as an atheist in Soviet Ukraine. When I described how we started the Bible Study to honor the Lord Jesus, the two attorneys who were Jewish (assuming that I was a Jewish immigrant from Kyiv) raised their voices at me. Their tone became belligerent saying, "how could you, being a Jew, betray your clan and become one of those guys who demeaned us here in our Saint Louis Park community. You don't know how we were ostracized here in Minneapolis not that long ago while you lived in your cozy Kyiv!" Cozy Kyiv-- Really?!?

Tom and Dave listened (Dave was seemingly praying for me knowing that I was a Gentile, but Tom, seeing that I was silent and did not disprove what was being said, probably, to this very day, thinks that I am Jewish). Well, Brother Tom, as you read this please know that I am Jewish in my heart to be sure. My parents and grandparents were Ukrainian/Polish, except for my maternal grandfather who was Persian Armenian. My BOSS for the past 41 years has unequivocally been the JEWISH CARPENTER Who is also known as the "King of the Jews," Jesus the Messiah, "despised and forsaken" by His own people, "pierced through for our transgressions" and, yes,"by His stripes we are healed" Isaiah 53:3,5.

"Thus, for my part, I am eager to preach the Gospel...for I am not ashamed of the Gospel, for it is the power of God for salvation to everyone who believes, TO THE JEW FIRST, and also to the Greek (Gentiles)" Romans 1:15,16.

Thank you, Prophet Isaiah, for being obedient in revealing the will of our Heavenly Father concerning His Son Jesus Christ in the short concise 12 verses of the Messianic chapter 53 of Isaiah. "By His knowledge the Righteous One, My Servant, will justify the many, (Heavenly Father is talking about His Son Jesus, the SERVANT), as He will bear their iniquities (Jesus bore the sins of mankind on the cross of Calvary); Therefore, I will allot Him a portion with the great, and He will divide the booty with the strong; Because He poured out Himself to death, and was numbered with the transgressors (crucified with two criminals); Yet He Himself bore the sin of many, and interceded for the transgressors" verses 11,12.

Here is the Biblical answer to a sadly common assumption that the Scripture is a fable written by mere men: "But know this first of all, that no prophecy of Scripture is a matter of one's own interpretation, for no prophecy was ever made by the act of human will, but men (like Prophet Isaiah) moved by the Holy Spirit spoke from God " 2 Peter 1:20,21.

I learned that the class action law suit involving age discrimination at IDS American Express was eventually won by the plaintiffs, and rightly so I might add..

Integrated Resources

Within a week of submitting my resignation letter and clearing my desk I received a call from Gene Goodner of Chattanooga,Tennessee, who invited me to speak to the members of his local church. I met Gene and his late darling wife Mary at the IDS President's Executive Council at the Ocean Reef Club, Key Largo, Florida in May of 1986.   Gene was one of the top financial planners nationally. He told me that after leaving IDS he became a Managing Executive for Integrated Resources, "a company of great potential", he said. As he described his new job he encouraged me to give it a try. "Victor, with your credentials, you will fit in. I will be praying for you."   Currently Gene Goodner is the Executive Director of the Master Financial Group in Chattanooga.   Each year I receive a small calendar from his office. Thank you, dear Brother, for putting a good word in for me 32 years ago. I will always remember that.

When I returned home I received a call from New York, from Mr. Geiger, who introduced himself as an Integrated Resources executive. He told me that he was aware of my accomplishments and invited me and Lilli to the company's headquarters in New York. "That way you will be able to better understand the scope of the company's operations and have firsthand knowledge of the services we provide. I am also a believer and pray that the Lord will show you the way," he said.

I accepted the offer and within a couple of days we were on our way to New York. Mr. Geiger was a very gracious host as he was explaining the various aspects of IREC's financial activities. He wanted me to move to New York considering thousands of Russian speaking immigrants who could use my services. "Your office will be in the second twin tower of the World Trade Center, we will go there tomorrow. You're going to like the view, it is stunning!" As I talked it over with Lilli she was reluctant to move saying, "it will be hard to leave my parents behind." We agreed that I would run my office from Minneapolis with occasional trips to New York.

Thank you Father for Your unfailing love and constant protection. King David asked You to "give ear to my words," "for to Thee do I pray. In the morning, O Lord, Thou wilt hear my voice; in the morning I will order my prayer to Thee and eagerly watch; return, O Lord, rescue my soul; save me because of Thy lovingkindness" Psalms 5:1,3. 6:4.

On the morning of Tuesday, September 11, 2001 nineteen members of the radical Islamic terrorist group Al-Qaeda launched a series of four coordinated terrorist attacks against the United States that killed 2,977 people and injured over 6,000 others, causing at least $10 billion in infrastructure and property damage. The second twin tower was among the casualties.

As a young father I changed professions from teaching to financial planning to provide for our growing family. (Our firstborn, Tania)

Chapter 9   MINISTRY WORK

Christian Business Men's Committee of the USA (CBMC)

In 1982, when I was working for IDS, I was invited by a Christian friend to attend the CBMC luncheon in Golden Valley. I gladly agreed. There I met a number of business and professional people. The atmosphere was relaxed, friendly and congenial. As we sat at the table, people talked about their business affiliation, family, and exchanged business cards. Then lunch was served and the host prayed and blessed the food. As we continued eating, the main speaker was introduced who briefly talked about his line of work and shared his testimony how Christian principles affected his life and business. He was very sincere when he shared with us his successes and failures. At the end he invited people to pray to receive the Lord. We filled out the cards in the middle of the table and several people indicated their first time decision to follow Christ (I learned later on). Three days later two gentlemen came to my cubicle at IDS and introduced themselves as members of the Golden Valley CBMC.

One of the men was Don Bania and the other Robert Williams, from Bobby and Steve's Auto World. "Victor, we were in the area and thought we'd stop by and say hello. Do you have a minute?" said Bobby. As we talked about the CBMC luncheon Bobby asked me a question: "Victor, have you come to a certain place in your spiritual life where you know for certain that if you were to die today you would go to heaven?" He also asked, " If you were to die today and stand before God and He asked why He should let you into heaven, what would you tell Him?" I was thrilled to answer those two questions! My answer was "IT IS ONLY BY THE AMAZING GRACE OF GOD THROUGH FAITH IN HIS

SON JESUS CHRIST, MY PERSONAL LORD AND SAVIOR, AM I ASSURED OF MY PLACE IN HEAVEN."

That same year I became a CBMC member. A little history: CBMC of the USA began in 1930 when a small group of Christian businessmen coordinated a series of pre-Easter prayer rallies. With the Great Depression in its second year these men saw an urgent need for spiritual revival and took it upon themselves to plan a six-week evangelistic series of meetings at the Garrick Theater in the Chicago loop area. Public response to the first gathering on January 6, 1931 was overwhelming as more than 800 packed into the 800-seat facility for all six sessions. As the meetings were drawing to a close, more and more men were experiencing life change through their new found relationship with Christ. It was determined that there was a need for a discipleship tool to help men ignite their walk with Jesus Christ. OPERATION TIMOTHY was created to be used for one-on-one applications where a MENTOR (whom we call PAUL) sits down with someone wishing to know more about God (TIMOTHY) and together they embark upon a transformational journey of exploring Christ's Word. CBMC members embrace two core beliefs: share the Gospel with those who do not know the Good News and then go and make disciples (to be intentional about carrying out the Great Commission).

Before His Ascension, Jesus said to his eleven disciples (Judas betrayed Jesus and hung himself, and Matthias was not chosen yet), "All authority has been given to me in heaven and on earth. Go therefore and make disciples of all the nations baptizing them in the name of the Father, and the Son, and the Holy Spirit. Teaching them to observe all that I commanded you and, lo, I am with you always, even to the end of the age" Matthew 28:18-20.

Witnessing to and discipling fellow business and professional people became an integral part of my professional career. I also became a regular speaker at the CBMC committees in the Twin Cities as well as at committees in other states sharing my testimony as a former Soviet atheist turned born-again Christian.

At that time the Minneapolis-St.Paul area had the most CBMC committees in the country, eighteen to be exact. We would regularly hold banquets, raising money to install Regional CBMC Directors locally and in other cities. Bobby Williams was the main facilitator and encourager along with other faithful brothers including Loren Helling, Dave Senger, Len Riley, Mike Haas, Wayne Sharp, John O'Sullivan, Jerry Cortem, Garry Dahle, Doug Cozad and many others. With several of the above mentioned CBMCers we formed a group called "The True Image" and traveled to New York, Milwaukee and Chicago, helping the local brothers set up CBMC Committees and install Regional Directors.

In 1988 Bobby Williams had a vision to have CBMC Committees in Jamaica. To that end he traveled to Kingston and Montego Bay on an exploratory trip and came back with encouraging news: "Brothers, the Lord showed me a great need for witnessing and discipleship of business and professional people in Jamaica! Local brethren asked us to come and help," he told our Golden Valley CBMC Committee. Our group prayed and sensed it was a "Macedonian call for help." In Acts 16 we read "And a vision appeared to Paul in the night: a certain man of Macedonia was standing and appealing to him, and saying,"Come over to Macedonia and help us." The text says that when Apostle Paul saw the vision he, along with Silas and Timothy, "Immediately sought to go into Macedonia, concluding that God had called us to preach the gospel to them" verses 9,10.

Within a short time we purchased our air tickets and, along with our wives, were on our way to Jamaica.

Bobby Williams with daughter, Melissa

Ivan Brown

Bobby told me that he talked to the brothers and they decided that I would be the main speaker at the CBMC banquet at Montego Bay. We prayed and asked for the Lord's leading. As I shared my testimony that fateful afternoon I noticed a tall, slender uniformed police officer listening intently, both his arms were fitted with prosthetics. Our eyes met several times as I presented the Gospel and gave an invitation to receive Jesus Christ. The next day Lenny Riley and I, as well as other brethren, went to see those who were in attendance at our CBMC banquet and who filled out their cards. We call it "Operation Shoe Leather." On one of the cards I saw the name "Ivan Brown" with the Police Precinct address. Lenny and I figured out it was the police officer we saw in attendance. It was a late afternoon when we took a taxi and went to find Ivan.

As we got out of the car and stood on the street not knowing where to go, we realized that we were the only "pale faces" as locals curiously observed us, some offering drugs. It was getting dark. We started praying for safety, asking Jesus to lead us to the Police Department. As we opened our eyes we saw officer Brown walking straight toward us! Now, I had experienced answers to prayer before in my Christian walk, but never such an instantaneous confirmation of Jesus' leading. Officer Brown was very surprised to see us (he later told us that no Americans, that he was aware of, had ventured to walk that far into the city AND that Lenny and I would have likely been mugged had he not walked down the street toward us. He also told us that he usually walked on a different street but that afternoon he decided to take a shortcut. I remember Lenny and I looking at each other realizing that we were on to something. Ivan told me that he recognized me from yesterday's banquet as we walked to his office.

Here is his incredible story of survival he shared with us. In July of 1975, when Ivan was a young 22 year old newly married police officer at Montego Bay, Jamaica, (his wife, Monica, was pregnant with their first child at the time), he went on a domestic disturbance call to a nearby ranch located close to the city limits. As he arrived at the destination he saw a drunk man with a machete (later identified as an escaped convict) chasing a panicking woman. Officer Brown pulled out his service revolver and ordered the suspect to freeze and put down his machete. When the suspect put down his machete on the floor, officer Brown proceeded to put his gun in the holster and started writing a citation. Unbeknownst to officer Brown, the suspect was hiding a second machete behind his back with which he attacked the officer, intending to decapitate him. Officer Brown tried to protect himself by extending his right arm which was severed "like a matchstick," Brown recalled. Then the suspect tried to hit the officer again at a different angle. This time the left arm was automatically raised for protection and instantaneously severed well above the elbow, also leaving a deep cut on Brown's forehead as it landed. The suspect dragged the semi conscious Ivan Brown into the field and left him there to die. Ivan remembered his last words before he blacked out, "Jesus, save me! Have mercy on me Christ, I will serve You if I live!" He was found by the patrol officer who traced the original call and was on his way to assist, as well as by the next door neighbor who heard the gunshot when the assailant took Ivan's gun and shot in the air.

Remarkably, some time earlier, Ivan had helped deliver the baby for that neighbor's wife who was the first on the scene before the ambulance came. The neighbor removed his shirt and made tourniquets trying to stop the extensive bleeding as they carried Ivan to his truck. Officer Brown almost "bled out." He vaguely remembered how his body rolled back and forth in excruciating pain in the back of the truck while racing down the bumpy road.

At the hospital, doctors tried to do their best to save Ivan's life by giving him several blood transfusions and all along wondering how he was still alive having lost so much blood. Ivan was later flown to London's Royal Hospital where he was fitted with prosthetics. His case was highly publicized as a "medical miracle."

As Lenny and I listened to his miraculous story, Ivan Brown fixed his gaze upon us and said, "the Lord has sent you two to collect on my promise to Jesus." I felt the presence of the Holy Spirit as I was explaining the plan of salvation to Ivan and leading him to Christ in prayer. We praised the Lord for the lost sheep that was found for eternity that unforgettable afternoon in Montego Bay. Brother Ivan gave us a ride to where we were staying, delivering us to our worried wives, Bonnie and Lilli.

Indeed the Lord God is the Lord of miracles and is "mighty to save" Isaiah 63:1. Ivan's wife, Monica, had a miscarriage when she learned about the tragedy. However, the Lord later blessed the Browns with two children, a boy and a girl. Superintendent Dr. Ivan Brown became a world class evangelist witnessing to "one and all" about the saving grace of our Wonderful Savior Jesus and testifying about his miraculous survival. In the editorial from the Jamaica Gleaner newspaper entitled "Beyond Cop's Disability," the editor reminisced, "We remember Ivan Brown whose name will forever be linked to police courage and survival. We refer to the late Superintendent Dr. Ivan Brown, from Western Jamaica, who was attacked by a suspect who severed both his arms. Despite the violence of the assault, Brown continued to serve after being fitted with prosthetics, and for years he was an inspiration within the JCF (Jamaica Constabulary Force) and to audiences across the world. His last assignment was Superintendent in charge of community relations in Area One."

In comments, Angela Mitchell wrote "I remember Ivan Brown very well. I remember the time I was still at school, he was a wonderful policeman, decent and well mannered. My grandma and other citizens of Westmoreland will tell you that we had one of the best policemen at the time."

Ivan Brown

The last time I had a chance to see this man of faith was in Minneapolis when he and his aide came to visit on the invitation of Bobby Williams who faithfully supported Ivan Brown and CBMC of Jamaica over the years. It was in the summer of 2004 if I am not mistaken. I remember taking Ivan and his aid on our boat on lake Minnetonka. He was enjoying the ride so much repeatedly saying "Aren't we blessed, Brother Victor! Aren't we truly blessed! Praise the Lord Jesus!" As I write this I have tears in my eyes remembering how thin Ivan was and yet how his face was radiating joy. He was thankful for being alive in Jesus Whom he served. He told me and Lilli that every time he shared his testimony he mentioned "Victor from Minneapolis, originally from Ukraine" who prayed with him to receive the Lord to "collect on his promise to Jesus." In 2007 Ivan went to be with the Lord Whom he loved. "The memory of the righteous is blessed" Proverbs 10:7.

The next time I see dear Brother Ivan Brown, he will be without prosthetics and it will be his turn to show me around "the city which has foundations, whose architect and builder is God" Hebrews 11:10.

Back In The USSR

In 1989, after 14 years of living in my newly adopted country, I came to quote the Beatles, "Back in the US..., back in the US..., back in the USSR." When Bobby challenged me to go back to the USSR he said "Pushkin, don't you want to tell your former countrymen about the love of Jesus?" (Brothers, can you just hear his voice calling me "Pushkin?" It was Bobby who assigned that nickname to me since he thought it sounded so Russian). Indeed it was--Alexander Pushkin was a great Russian poet 1799-1837).

Initially, I replied, "but Bobby, they will do something bad to me AGAIN, remember they declared me insane and wanted to give me an injection of turpentine to kill me! They told me to never come back. Plus now, having four small children, Lilli would never let me go!" To which he replied "who are you afraid of?" "If God is with us, who is against us?" check Romans 8:31. I did. It was there. That settled that.

My dear Brother Bobby Williams, fearless and compassionate follower of Christ, was used by God to encourage me and Lilli to go back to my native country for which I am very thankful. Lilli and I organized a trip for our fellow CBMC members: Bobby Williams and his daughter Mellisa; Dave and Karen Senger; Loren and Betty Helling; Harry and Diana Evert; George and Debbie Sontowski (George is Lilli's brother); and Slavko and Oksana Billy.

Little did I know at the time that the Lord would call me to the office of an evangelist and give me the opportunity to travel to Ukraine, Russia, Moldova, Belarus and Slovenia more than seventy times over the next 30 years. Thank you, Jesus. Like a New Testament Barnabas (son of exhortation), Bobby continued to encourage, pray and support my ministry over the years. He traveled with me to Ukraine several times.

So, in the summer of 1989 I travelled back to my former homeland. Our group visited Moscow, Kyiv, Kharkiv and Odessa preaching the Gospel everywhere we went, gathering scores of people who were eager to hear the Word of God. In Moscow, on Red Square we were passing out "Four Spiritual Laws" tracts to the guards who were marching to the Lenin Mausoleum. On another Red Square, in Kharkiv, we were preaching the Gospel for many hours (one of us would present the Gospel and extend the invitation to receive Jesus, then another would share his testimony as new people would come to listen). We had a great time in Kyiv and Odessa, meeting and witnessing to my uncle's family, to former friends and musicians; leading them to Christ while Jesus was "adding day by day those who were being saved" Acts 2:47.

The Lord showed me way back then that the Soviet people who had been living in Communist darkness without hope for over 70 years were hungry for the Word of God. I also sensed that the Lord was calling me back to my native country to preach the Gospel of Salvation. People were ready to receive the Good News.

I should mention that on our return flight from Frankfurt to America we were told by the flight attendant that the plane's baggage compartment door was not hermetically sealed and that the pilot would have to return to Germany to attempt an emergency landing. I saw how the jet fuel was streaming from the plane's wings as the pilot tried to dump as much fuel as needed to prevent an explosion on impact. We all prayed for safety and the Lord's protection for all of us on the plane and for our children back home, being confident that even if we do not make it our Savior will take care of them according to His promise, "I will never desert you, nor will I ever forsake you" Hebrews 13:5b. People on the plane became hysterical. Many were openly crying. The lady sitting next to us was frantically repeating the Lord's prayer and "Hail Marys" over and over, holding her rosary in her trembling hands. Lord knows, our group was calm and contemplative, trusting the Lord for the outcome. We landed safely with loud "Hallelujahs" from all the members of the group. Within a short time we were on our way from Frankfurt to Minneapolis again, praising the Lord for His goodness and mercy that followed us on that memorable trip to Ukraine.

Gorbachev's Visit To Minneapolis

In March of 1990 I received a call from John Tschohl, President of Better Than Money Corp., a local consumer and educational services company. He told me that a "Russian dignitary" was in town and that he wanted me to be an interpreter that same afternoon for lunch at the Governor's mansion in Saint Paul. My first thought was, "it's probably one of those typical old, repulsive bureaucrats like I had interpreted for many times before." Nevertheless, I reluctantly agreed. As I arrived at the Governor's mansion John introduced me to Governor Rudy Perpich, his beautiful wife Delores (Lola), and Oleg Uralov, the tall, handsome, athletic, blue-eyed Scandinavian looking "Russian dignitary" with a broad smile. Shockingly surprising.

As I later spoke with Oleg (he insisted I call him by his first name) I found out he had been a Moscow swimming champion specializing in the backstroke. The Lord gave me liking in his eyes as I told him about the U.S. Olympic swimmer Mark Spitz who visited my native Kyiv in the 1980s.

Mr. Uralov was Director General of Video Film Corporation and a Deputy Chairman of the State Committee of the USSR for Cinematography. He was also a biographer of Raisa Gorbachev, wife of the USSR

President Mikhail Gorbachev. During lunch Governor Perpich was telling Mr. Uralov about the USSR - Minnesota Connect Program. "Minnesota is the leading state of the Union that has broad cultural and business relations with your country," he told Mr. Uralov. As I was speaking Russian with Oleg (while the Governor took an important call), I mentioned that it would be great for Mr. Gorbachev and his wife Raisa to visit Minnesota, the land of 10,000 lakes--Minnesota nice, you know. Governor Perpich asked me what I had said to Oleg since he heard Gorbachev's name mentioned. I told him that it would be nice to have the Russian Premier visit our state since he would be in Washington DC for the Summit meeting with President Bush Senior and then flying to San-Francisco. "Gorbachev could stop by Minnesota on the way," I told the Governor. "Victor, if Gorby comes to Minnesota and I am reelected, you will be my Lieutenant Governor" said Rudy semi jokingly. I kind of liked that idea.

Governor Perpich, Oleg Uralov, Lola Perpich

Governor Perpich initiated the visit with an invitation to Mikhail and Raisa Gorbachev followed by lobbying from business leaders. On an unusually chilly and blustery Sunday, June 3rd, 1990, Soviet Premier Gorbachev arrived for a short seven hour visit to

Minnesota that underscored the thaw in the Cold War. Within eighteen months the Soviet Union collapsed followed by Gorbachev's resignation. No political observer or writer could have predicted such a drastic historic change-- no one but God Almighty, Creator of heavens and earth, "It is He Who sits above the vault of the earth, HE it is who reduces rulers to nothing, Who makes the judges of the earth meaningless" Isaiah 40: 22, 23. "And it is He Who changes the times and the epochs: He removes kings and establishes kings" Daniel 2:21.

The eighth and last leader of the Soviet Union, the General Secretary of its governing Communist Party from 1985 until 1991, Gorbachev initiated changes known as perestroika and glasnost which melted the rigid godless Soviet system and liberated 15 Soviet Republics to become independent states. Thus ended the existence of, as President Reagan aptly termed it, the "Evil Empire" December, 1991.

I vividly remember being interviewed by local WCCO TV anchor Pat Miles during Gorbachev's visit to the Twin Cities. The title on the TV screen was "Victor Branitski. Practicing Christianity." My good friend and brother in Christ, Dave S, commented back then, "it's like you are practicing some sort of a cult." I told Pat how Christians were persecuted in the USSR for their faith in Jesus Christ and how the true "perestroika" (rebuilding) of PEOPLES' HEARTS is needed in my former land. "Unless the Lord builds the house,
They labor in vain who build it" Psalm 127:1.

You might be wondering about my promised lucrative political future. After all, the Gorbachevs did come to town. Unfortunately, Governor Perpich lost the election to his rival Arnie Carlson which put a serious damper on my Lieutenant Governorship. Bummer. After leaving office in 1991, Rudy Perpich went to Zagreb,

Croatia, as U.S. Ambassador to assist its post-communist government. He died in 1995 at the age of 67.

Crusades With Evangelist John Guest In Russia And Ukraine

In 1990 I was serving on the Board of Slavic Gospel Association, Wheaton, Illinois. Peter Deyneka was the SGA President and the son of the legendary evangelist, "Peter Dynamite" whose motto was "Much prayer, much power. Little prayer, little power. No prayer, no power." I was contacted by the John Guest Evangelistic Team regarding organizing and holding large scale crusades in Ukraine with a side trip to Moscow. The purpose of the trip was to present the Gospel to large audiences of people, plant new churches and prepare young church leaders to carry out The Great Commission. The well-known evangelist and pastor, Dr. John Guest, born in Oxford, England and now residing in Sewickley, Pennsylvania, was the main speaker. His lovely wife, Kathy, and daughters accompanied him on the trip.

John's testimony goes back in time when he was invited by a friend to hear the American evangelist Billy Graham in London in 1954. John was 18 at the time, studying engineering. That fateful night he responded to God's call and made his commitment to Jesus Christ. Shortly thereafter John felt God calling him into full time service as a pastor.

Speaking about London--Lilli and I visited this beautiful city in the early 1990s on the invitation of a dear Christian couple, Peter and Faith Loose who were connected with the John Guest Evangelistic Team. Brother Peter is well known and respected in British evangelical circles. He arranged a number of speaking engagements for me in and around Chelmsford and at

126

London's Westminster Chapel where I met the late Dr. R.T. Kendall, American Baptist Pastor.

Peter Loose

Dr. Kendall

Dr. Kendall believed that the Gospel needed to be applied and spoken with a penetrating directness in an increasingly atheistic, secularized and materialistic society.

The 1990 John Guest team to Ukraine and Russia included Christian musician Leon Patillo (former keyboardist, composer and arranger for the rock group Santana) as well as a popular Christian singer, Deneen Alexandrow, from the famous Christ Church Choir, Nashville, Tennessee.

Deneen is an American of Russian - Ukrainian descent. She performed a number of Christian songs that Lilli and I translated from English into Russian and Ukrainian. She subsequently recorded the first contemporary Christian album in Ukraine with the world famous Revutsky Academic Male Ukrainian Choir under the renowned conductor Bohdan Antkiv in the summer of 1991. The album became an immediate bestseller.

Christian businessman, Clare DeGraaf, author of "The Ten Second Rule," and my coordinator in Kyiv, Vladimir Zybin, were negotiating with the management of the Dynamo Soccer Team regarding renting Dynamo stadium for our crusades. Even though it was not easy to deal with the Soviet secular officials, we still felt the hand of God in everything that was arranged. I remember dear brother Clare leaving for the US after a series of long and frustrating negotiations with the Ukrainian "partners" exclaiming with a sigh of relief, "I am free, I am free indeed!" I smile remembering him saying it in front of the Dnipro hotel hurrying to catch a flight to the good old USA.

With John Guest, Clare DeGraaf, Volodia Zybin

Thank you, Clare, (and another brother, Rich Correll), for all you did in planning and arranging that highly successful, FIRST TIME IN KYIV, historic, mass scale evangelistic crusade. You truly exercised the fourth gift of the Holy Spirit in Galatians 5:22--PATIENCE! May our merciful Savior Jesus richly bless you and keep you strong in our common faith as we are "looking for the blessed hope and the appearing of the glory of our great God and Savior, Christ Jesus" Titus 2:13.

Meanwhile, John Guest, filled with the Holy Spirit, preached "with boldness the mystery of the Gospel," Ephesians 6:19 everywhere we went, inviting people to repent and receive Jesus, the soon coming King of kings and Lord of lords. I was John's interpreter and associate evangelist sharing my testimony of coming "from darkness into His marvelous light." We sensed people's deep spiritual hunger for the Word of God after over seventy years of communist anti-Christian propaganda. It was now Jesus' time to be proclaimed openly in Kyiv, the city with over 1,500 year history.

Open air concerts and outreaches at the Arch, Kyiv

John Guest

Legend has it, as written by Nestor The Scribe, that Apostle Andrew, the first called disciple of Christ, (*Первозванний*), patron saint of Ukraine, preached in the lands of Rus where Scythian tribes lived. Once, before reaching a mountain, he placed a cross and prophesied great glory to the city which would some day arise. Kyiv, the heart of Ukraine, was formed 500 years later.

Apostle Paul knew about Scythians. Writing to the church of Colossae he encouraged believers to "put on the new self who is being renewed to a true knowledge according to the image of the One Who created him - a renewal in which there is no distinction between Greek and Jew, circumcised and uncircumcised, barbarian, SCYTHIAN, slave and freeman, but Christ is all and in

131

all" Colossians 3:10,11. (The famous Scythian gold was found at Ukrainian Trypillya. There is a museum of Scythian gold in Kyiv featuring unique gold jewelry including the famous gold necklace dating 2,500 years B.C.).

St Vladimir Hill commemorates Christianity in Kyiv since 988 AD

During our crusades, the interest in spiritual values was simply overwhelming as hundreds of people flocked to our outreaches where we were preaching the Word of God, distributing Christian literature, and calling people to come forward for the prayer of repentance. The Lord powerfully used Deneen and Leon to proclaim Christ in music and song.

The stereotype of Christianity being typically viewed as old uneducated "babushkas" with scarfs on their heads was significantly altered as people heard John's preaching, him being a Doctor of Theology. The people thoroughly enjoyed and were inspired by our dear talented musicians glorifying the Lord Jesus with upbeat songs of praise. The John Guest support group traveling with us was actively sharing the Gospel and encouraging Ukrainians to look up to Jesus, the only hope for Ukraine. All in all, the Lord Jesus was proclaimed in Kyiv, the capital of Ukraine, with a population close to three million, day in and day out for a few weeks. As a result, several new churches were organized from hundreds of new converts.

Preaching at the Dynamo Kyiv Soccer Stadium

Moscow's Gorky Park

In Moscow John Guest spoke at the well-known Gorky Park theater and the famous Arbat street. Hundreds of people heard the saving message of Jesus with scores of first time decisions to accept Christ. He also addressed the historic Moscow Central Baptist Church where Billy Graham spoke earlier in the 1980s.

With John Guest on Arbat Street, Moscow

Return To Kyiv With Astronaut

The evangelical leadership of Ukraine, witnessing the spiritual revival in the land and keen interest in Christianity, invited the John Guest Evangelistic Team to return the following year to conduct a series of outreaches and workshops to prepare young Christian leaders to carry out the Great Commission. For the next two years, 1991 and 1992, the John Guest Team returned to Ukraine for more evangelistic outreaches that included Kyiv, Vinnitsa, Slavutych, Pripyat and Chernobyl. This time our guest speaker was the NASA Astronaut, Brigadier General Charles Duke who was a Lunar Module pilot of Apollo 16 in April of 1972. He became the tenth and youngest person at age 36 to walk on the lunar surface.

Charlie and his wife Dotty are committed born-again Christians and along with John Guest they were sharing with Ukrainians their unshakable faith in the Lord Jesus Christ. What a privilege it was for me to serve these men of God as their interpreter. Their unforgettable testimonies of courage, faithfulness and dedication to our Savior are forever etched in my mind.

Charlie came to the saving faith in Christ in 1978 at a Bible study (it was a good year, Brother, I also came to Jesus in 1978). In his presentation he used these two verses to describe the majesty of the Almighty God, the Creator of Heavens and Earth: "He stretches out the north over empty space and hangs the earth on nothing" Job 26:7. "It is He who sits above the vault ('knug' in Hebrew which means 'round') of the earth" Isaiah 40:22. "I witnessed the stunning beauty of planet Earth walking on the moon when I lifted my head straight up and in utter darkness observed the perfectly round jewel that looked like a changing color diamond. Our Earth is fascinating!" Charlie would say.

Astronaut, Charles Duke

Chernobyl

Here is an incredible story about how the Lord made it possible for our team to preach Christ in Chernobyl, 500 feet away from Nuclear Reactor Number Four. The Chernobyl nuclear disaster occurred on Saturday, April 26th, 1986 at the Number Four nuclear reactor of the Chernobyl Nuclear Power Plant near the city of Pripyat, 84 miles north of Kyiv. It is considered the worst nuclear disaster in history and is one of only two nuclear energy disasters rated at seven (the maximum severity) on the International Nuclear Event Scale. The other being the 2011 Fukushima Daiichi Nuclear disaster in Japan.

In July of 1991 John Guest and I were walking down Khreschatyk Street where the City Hall and Mayor's Office is situated. Earlier I showed John Pushkinskaya Street where I had lived for 27 years before immigrating to the US in 1975. As we were approaching the City Hall, John asked me if we could see the City Mayor. (At that time the Mayor of Kyiv was Mykola Kosachivsky).

"Victor, let's get the Mayor's permission to go to Chernobyl and tell the nuclear plant personnel about Jesus! They need encouragement!" John said with the conviction and enthusiasm that only he could exhibit. "But, John, don't you think we, at the very least, would need an appointment? Plus how could we get in without a special pass (propusk)? There are armed guards at the entrance door, you know!" I said in disbelief. "Victor, my brother, Jesus will get us through. Let's walk in the power of the Holy Spirit. Remember there is nothing impossible for God. Let's pray."

We did and I told John that I am entering into his faith (mine was lacking at the time). He prayed a fervent prayer to the One Whose power and authority are infinite. As we walked to the City Hall, John was the first to open the door and face the armed guard who asked him to produce the pass. John, towering 6'6," smiled and told the guard that he wanted to see the Mayor. He obviously spoke his royal British English which the guard could not understand. *Пропуск, пропуск! Покажите Ваш пропуск!* (show your pass) the guard yelled thinking that if he yelled loud enough in Russian John could understand him. Before I could open my mouth to interpret, the man standing behind me, looking very official, told the guard to let us through. "They probably want to go to the International Department (*международный отдел*)," he told the guard. "It is on the second floor," he told John in English. John and I looked at each other realizing that Jesus was on it--big time.

As we walked to the second floor I noticed the door with a sign: Vladimir Melnik, Head of the International Department. "Wait a minute, I remember this name" I told John. "I studied at the University of Kyiv with Vladimir Melnik. Could that be a coincidence?" I knocked on the door. Hearing "come in," we entered the office. Sitting at the big ministerial table was none other than Vladimir, my buddy from the university. He rushed to meet us saying, "Brunya, (my nickname) I can't believe it! I tried to find you. I saw John Guest and you on the news the other day speaking at Dynamo Stadium. And here you are!" We hugged and then I introduced John.

"How did you get here? What can I do for you?" Vladimir asked. My dear brother John looked at me somewhat suspiciously. Now he was, no doubt, thinking that the whole thing was prearranged by me in the first place. It was such a precious funny moment when John asked "Victor, did you do it?" I answered "absolutely not, it is Jesus! Remember, we prayed." It makes me smile while writing this--yes, it was the Lord! John told Vladimir (who spoke fluent English) that we wanted to meet the Mayor and ask his permission to visit Chernobyl.

Vladimir told us that Mayor Kosachivsky would be in the office the next day and suggested we come back by 11:00 a.m. "I will personally meet you at the guard desk," he said. I told Vladimir that we would bring the Astronaut, Charles Duke, with us. "That would be great!" he said. "The Mayor would love to see the Man who walked on the Moon!"

When we returned to our hotel we asked our group to pray about our appointment with the Mayor. Everybody was very encouraged. Matthew 19:26 records the words of our Savior, "With men this is impossible, but with God all things are possible." Prayer works!

The next morning John, Charlie, and yours truly met the excited Mayor and Vladimir to discuss our trip to Chernobyl. As we entered his office the Mayor gave all three of us big bear hugs as if we had known each other for a long time (the other night our team prayed that the Lord would give us favor in the Mayor's eyes just like He "extended kindness" to Joseph "and gave him favor in the sight of the chief jailer" in Genesis 39:21). The Mayor explained that the radiation at Chernobyl Nuclear Plant was still high. (Radiation dose depends on three factors: the strength of the radiation source, the distance you are from it, and the duration of the exposure. The average exposure from all radiation sources for a member of the public is approximately 0.28 uSv/hr. Nuclear workers are subjected to a 3 - 25 uSv/hr. range). Also there was a 40 kilometer Forbidden Zone surrounding Chernobyl and at that point NOBODY was allowed to cross it. The Mayor said that he would make an exception for the John Guest group and turning to me asked, "Victor, do you really want to go?" (*Подумай, это опасно*)! "Think about it, it is dangerous!" We prayed about it and trusted the Lord for the outcome. It was a unique opportunity to share Jesus with hundreds of people and we asked the Lord for protection.

While talking to the Mayor, John Guest said that he wanted to invite him, Vladimir, and Kyiv District Mayors (15 of them) with wives for dinner the next day before our trip to Chernobyl. "Charlie Duke will share his experience walking on the moon", he said. "Could you give us the phone numbers of the mayors so that we could invite them personally?" John asked the Mayor. The Mayor smiled in return and said "don't waste your time calling" and then phoned his secretary in our presence, commanding, "tomorrow, at the Hotel National Banquet Hall at 18 hours (6:00 pm) all mayors are invited with their wives for dinner given by MY AMERICAN FRIENDS. All mayors are obliged, without fail, to be present!" "That's the way we do things here," he told me.

The next day, at the luxurious private dining hall of the famous National Hotel located at Pechersky District, we met (you guessed it) ALL 15 Kyiv District Mayors with their wives headed by the proud Mayor of Kyiv, Mykola Kosachivsky, and his wife. The scenario was written in heaven. The Lord gave us favor in their eyes as John and Charlie were witnessing about the love of God and His amazing creation. I should mention that before dinner Charlie Duke suggested that we all bow our heads and give thanks for the food. Everyone was waiting for the Mayor's reaction. He was the first to bow his head in prayer. ALL the Mayors obediently followed. At that time several waitresses started walking into the dining room with hors d'oeuvres and literally froze observing over 50 people praying, INCLUDING THE MAYOR.

The Lord Jesus was glorified and at the end John offered the salvation prayer. It was obvious our guests were moved by the sincerity and Christian love coupled by the incredible story of Charlie's odyssey to the moon and back. When we said our final goodbyes the Mayor had tears in his eyes thanking the John Guest Evangelistic Team and Charlie and Dotty Duke for "opening our eyes and hearts to the Gospel." Praise the Lord for His invisible and yet tangible presence that night. The precious "seed" was planted.

Road to Chernobyl

The next morning, Friday, July 12, our team set out for our 84 mile historic trip to Chernobyl. We stopped at the abandoned ghost city of Pripyat on the way which is near the Ukraine Belarus border. Pripyat was founded in 1970 as the ninth nuclear city (a type of "closed city") in the USSR to serve the nearby Chernobyl Nuclear Power Plant. It was an eerie sight to see the former city of nearly 50,000 completely overtaken by wild vegetation (the city was evacuated in April, 1986). We also visited the city of Slavutych, sparsely populated, where we preached the Gospel. We noticed that the emblem of the city looked like the darkened sun with a star above and black waves beneath. The local mayor explained to us that the imagery was taken from the Book of Revelation, Chapter 8, where the fallen big star, Wormwood, (in Ukrainian "Chernobyl") fell from heaven on one third of the rivers and springs of waters like a burning torch making waters bitter, verses 10-12.

Chernobyl

When we finally arrived at the Chernobyl Nuclear Power Plant we were greeted by the plant manager and head engineers of the 3rd and 5th nuclear reactors. They told us that several hundred workers were waiting for us at the local soccer field that was about 500 feet away from the 4th reactor that blew up. Plant management provided us with a flatbed truck covered with a rug that served as the podium.

Chernobyl, 500 feet from the 4th Nuclear Reactor

Nearby we noticed grass as tall as the soccer goal post and yet yards away it seemed to be normal. They told us that radiation is spotty (we noticed that when we were driving from Kyiv through the woods seeing very lush vegetation in one spot and very sparse in another). We were also told that the radioactive contamination is the strongest in the woods. Thinking back, I can't but thank Jesus for protecting our team since it took us over two hours to get to Chernobyl through the woods of Ukraine and Belarus.

As Charlie Duke shared his testimony of his incredible experience of walking on the moon, and John Guest powerfully preached on assurance of eternal life through Christ alone, we noticed that black clouds started gathering on the horizon. We looked at each other and started praying that the Lord would hold back the rain until after John gave an invitation to receive Jesus (I should mention that we brought expensive sound equipment that we rented from Finland and were afraid the rain would ruin it). The Lord held back the rain! Almost all in the audience raised their hands to make a first time decision to follow Christ. And only then did the showers of blessing pour out on the happy faces of the redeemed of the Lord. To God be the glory! (The sound man was able to cover the speakers and the board).

When the rain stopped as abruptly as it had started and we said our final goodbyes, men were seemingly moved. One by one they came to shake our hands and thank us for visiting them. We all sensed the presence of Jesus Christ Who through the Holy Spirit, the True Comforter, encouraged those true sacrificial heroes to look up to Him, the Author and Perfecter of our faith. The final verse of encouragement we left with them was from Matthew 28:20. Jesus speaking, "...and lo, I am with you always, even to the end of the age."

143

After that we went to visit a small village within the so-called "40 Kilometer Zone." We had explicit authorization from the Kyiv Mayor. After the Chernobyl explosion, April 26,1986, the authorities closed off several small villages in the 40 kilometer radius from the existing world. Not even the members of immediate family were allowed to come and visit their dying aged parents. It's pretty much like what is happening nowadays at our hospitals and nursing homes with COVID-19 patients.

In preparation for our visit, the Kyiv authorities called that particular village director and told him that "if the John Guest Evangelistic Team is not tired after visiting Pripyat, Slavutych and Chernobyl, they might stop by for a short visit." The villagers waited for hours to see new human faces after five years of strict isolation. Even though everyone was very tired after several hours of emotionally charged meetings and fasting, we could not miss that once in a lifetime opportunity. We sensed the Lord's strong leading as we arrived an hour later to be greeted by the openly emotional folks dressed in their finest attire. Men wore military orders and medals from World War II on their civilian suit coats. A number of them were highly decorated. I remember one man in his seventies wearing three Orders of Glory (*Орден Славы*) for extraordinary combat gallantry (three Orders of Glory equals a golden medal of the Hero of the Soviet Union).Women likewise had military decorations and were dressed in beautifully hand embroidered outfits. The village director told me that "the Savior Himself brought you to us. We are abandoned by everybody" *(сам Спас привів вас до нас. ми всіми покинуті)*. He also told me that over half the village population, or approximately 85 people, had passed away and the rest are expected to follow shortly in the near future. I was fighting tears. In moments like those the Gospel of Christ seemed to have an even stronger power, conviction and encouragement.

The message we brought them was from John 11:25,26: "Jesus said to her (Martha), I am the resurrection and the life, he who believes in Me shall live even if he dies, and everyone who lives and believes in Me shall never die. Do you believe this?" All the villagers indicated their decision to recommit their lives afresh and trust Jesus for their salvation. As we were leaving we prayed that the Lord would sustain these precious folks and that someday we would see each other in heaven. (By 1995 all villages in the "40 Kilometer Chernobyl Forbidden Zone" ceased to exist). "For if we believe that Jesus died and rose again, even so God will bring with Him those who have fallen asleep in Jesus" 1 Thessalonians 5:14.

Slavic Gospel Association

Shortly after John Guest's Crusades in Ukraine I was asked by the then President of SGA, Dr. John Aker, to join the Association as an Executive Director of Evangelism and Discipleship in the Commonwealth of Independent States (CIS). Being an SGA Board Member, I prayerfully agreed. It involved mass preaching and discipleship of new believers as well as seminars and workshops for church leaders. John was a great encourager. He had served in the U.S. Army for 20 years, was a senior pastor of several evangelical churches, and authored several books and articles. John continues to serve people, currently running the highly rated Aker Kasten Home Health Care service in Palm Beach, Florida along with his brother Dr.Allen Aker.

Reflections

Read John Aker's "Reflections" article in the addendum

Masked Gunmen In Moscow

In the winter of 1994, John Aker, Tom Clinton (SGA's Vice-President, pastor and former missionary to the Philippines), Wendy Griffith (TV anchor from Rockford, Illinois, currently co-host for CBN's The 700 Club and a senior correspondent for Christian Broadcasting Network), a cameraman, and yours truly visited Moscow on a mission's trip. After speaking at Moscow State University about American Judeo-Christian values and the Gospel of Christ we strolled down the famous Kutuzov Prospect hoping to find a cafe to warm up and have a cup of coffee. Wendy was wearing a Russian fox fur hat and looked like a movie star. She certainly was the center of attention as people stared at her and her "accompanying entourage" (that is us, the three bodyguards).

However Wendy was not destined to be the only celebrity that afternoon. Let me explain. Former President Bill Clinton was in Moscow at the same time holding talks with Russian President Boris Yeltsin January 12-15. It was then that Clinton's secret service agents were rescued by helicopter from the InterContinental Hotel roof where they were stranded when the exit door unexpectedly closed behind them and they stood the chance of being frozen to death. We are talking about the harsh Russian winter. So, when I introduced Tom Clinton to the University students they assumed that Tom was President Clinton's brother. Tom is tall like President Clinton who is 6'2" and fits the image perfectly. Students rushed up to Tom after our presentation to get his autograph. He realized what was happening and played along signing their student IDs and passports "Clinton--John 3:16". Thus, Tom was a "co-celebrity" with Wendy that memorable freezing afternoon in Moscow.

Now, fast forward to the frightening event that is not easily forgotten. We finally found a nice cafe and sat at the table at the end of a long corridor. It was a "happening place"-- we noticed a number of young couples chatting, enjoying their coffee and tea with delicious looking pastries. The atmosphere was cheerful. We were in a celebratory mood ourselves recalling our experience at the University and praising the Lord for His leading. I noticed several well dressed, rowdy young people in black leather jackets sitting at the table near us. They were loud, drinking champagne and acting very cavalier. My back was facing the entrance door, some 50-60 feet away. Wendy was sitting in front of me, John to the left and Tom to the right. I could not see who was entering the cafe, the other three could. Suddenly Wendy whispered "Oh, my Lord!", her face turning pale. There was immediate silence in the cafe. Tom started hiding his money pouch behind his back. I remember saying, "what's happening?" John whispered, "Victor, turn around! Who are those guys?" As I turned around, still not understanding what was going on, I saw what seemed to be a dozen masked gunmen with AK-47s drawn, spreading rapidly around the perimeter of the cafe. They were dressed in fatigues and one of them shouted, "hands and passports on the table! Now!" Everyone was terrified. Within a split second one of the gunmen rushed to our table. I noticed a small round insignia on the gunman's left sleeve. "OMON," I read--"special police unit" (these guys are ruthless and usually deal with organized crime). When I reached for my passport which was in my jacket pocket the gunman directed his weapon straight between my eyes saying, "don't move!" At that point I told him that we were American missionaries who came to share about the love of Jesus. I also told him that I was a former first lieutenant. I saw through his eye mask holes that he smiled. At that moment the Lord gave me complete peace. We were fresh out of The Four Spiritual Laws tracts otherwise I could have rolled it up to put it in the muzzle of his gun.

Now you might want to ask me why OMON police came to our cafe. Remember that table near us with men dressed in black jackets? They happened to be Russian mafia. That is who the police were after. When the police cuffed both the men and the women sitting at the table they confiscated several guns and large sums of American currency. I'd say no more champagne in the foreseeable future for those thugs.

We prayed and thanked the Lord for His divine protection. Think about it--if the Mafia table had decided to open fire we would have been in the line of fire. Again, thank You, Jesus!

Minnesota Baptist Conference
Special Surprise Breakfast In Smila

In the late 1990s the Director of the Minnesota Baptist Conference, Dr.Truett Lawson, and I were visiting the Ukrainian town of Smila in Cherkasy Region as part of the Sister Church Program involving MBC churches and the Ukrainian Evangelical Baptist Union. Local pastors asked me if Truett liked fish to which I replied, "of course he does, after all, Minnesota is the land of 10,000 lakes and our state fish is the walleye."

The next morning, before breakfast, the senior pastor, his face radiating with joy, told me that several church members went fishing at dawn that morning specifically to catch fish for the American guests. "They prayed and caught a lot of fish for our dear American brothers. But it is a surprise, don't tell Truett." Truett was seated as the honored guest and was served the "special" bowl of fish soup. Looking up at him was a monstrous carp head. The eyes of the carp were looking straight at Truett. Truett's reaction was priceless, "Victor, do I really have to eat it?" I tried to be as serious as possible while suppressing my laughter at the shocked expression on Truett's face. Having gotten up at six a.m., praying for success, the brethren were so joyful to have caught the fish for him. "Truett, if you do not eat it you will definitely hurt their feelings." I suppose it would have been nice of me to offer to switch bowls with him, but this scenario was just too funny. Well, it wasn't exactly a walleye dinner, but it's the thought that counts. For the longest time we chuckled about this story recalling Truett's trip to Ukraine.

The Sister Church project which partnered American churches with churches in Ukrainian cities and villages was very successful as the Lord kept encouraging Ukrainian believers and their American counterparts to look up to Him for answers. New churches were built across the entire Cherkasy Region with the help of faithful American believers. Thousands of Ukrainians experienced a personal relationship with God. In Zolotonosha and other cities and villages Bible camps were established which are functioning to this very day. A dear Christian couple from Calvary Baptist in Roseville, Dr. Paul and Linda Wicklund, were involved with this greatly appreciated project from the very start, sacrificially supporting and encouraging Ukrainian believers. Pastor Rich Schoenert's teaching at Kremenchug Seminary was invaluable for Ukrainian church leaders. As MBC coordinator, I had the privilege of traveling with them and several other sister church groups from Minnesota. Our trips together have enriched me with beautiful, lasting memories.

Grace Slavic Church of Eagan

In the late 1990s a group of Russian evangelical Christians asked me to help plant a new Slavic church with the emphasis on reaching the unchurched immigrants in the Twin Cities. They asked me to co-pastor the church. I told them I was happy to help for an initial period of six months (which in actuality turned out to be thirteen years). Since I had a Masters in Pastoral Studies from Odessa Bible College I agreed to be a volunteer pastor. In time we purchased a church building in Eagan with the help of a number of our American friends, including a generous donation from Bobby Williams. We had outreaches for the Russian Jewish community. More and more immigrants from the former Soviet Union were learning about the historic God of Abraham, Isaac and Jacob who revealed Himself in His Son Jesus, the Messiah. It was a blessing to serve this growing church where over 70 percent were unchurched newcomers eager to hear the Word of God.

Grace Slavic Church outdoor baptism service

Our boys' baptism day

On several occasions I took people from our church to Ukraine on mission trips. One such trip was with Pavel Ness, our music director. We brought humanitarian aid and shared the Gospel in seven cities of central and eastern Ukraine (Kyiv, Bila Tserkva, Gorlovka, Yenakievo, Donetsk, Shevchenkovo, and

Odessa). The purpose of the trip was to share the Gospel with a broad spectrum of unchurched people, as well as to encourage local churches and home Bible study groups to continue to evangelize and disciple new believers. The Lord graciously allowed us to accomplish what we had planned and much more. The verse from Ephesians 3:20 came into a fresh and new light as we observed Jesus in action, "now to Him, Who is able to do exceeding abundantly beyond all that we ask or think, according to the power that works within us, to Him be the glory in the church and in Christ Jesus to all generations forever and ever, Amen!"

Munira's Escape From An Honor Killing

I would like to relate the unbelievable testimony of a young lady who visited our church in Eagan. I will never forget the story of this godly young woman from the former Soviet Republic of Tajikistan. Munira grew up as the only daughter in a traditional Muslim family. Her father was a military colonel and mother a teacher. Her grandfather was a local Imam which in Arabic means "leader," "model." He and his wife loved and cherished their only granddaughter from infancy.

When American missionaries came to their town, Munira and her teenage girlfriends attended the meeting. She described how she first heard about the love of Jesus and His death on the cross for the sins of the world. When the missionary spoke about Christ's resurrection and the need to know Him personally, Munira sincerely prayed to receive the Lord Jesus in her heart. She told us how happy she was to be forgiven and how she wanted to share her newly found faith with her family. When she came home that fateful night, excited to share the Good News with her family (the grandparents lived in the same house with her), her grandfather beat her, trying to force her to deny Jesus. She refused. They tied her to a chair and told her that if she did not change her mind by the next morning she would be killed for denouncing her Muslim faith.

Her older brother was supposed to cut her throat in public as "an honor or shame killing." According to a 2000 report from the UNFPA (United Nations Population Fund) an estimated 5,000 "honor" killings are committed every year, mostly in Muslim, Hindu and Sikh communities around the world. But the number could in fact be far higher because the killings are frequently not reported to authorities by the victims' families. The Department of Justice commissioned report in May 2015 indicated that an estimated 23 to 27 "honor" killings occur in the U.S. per year. In 2010, for example, Faleh Almaleki, an Iraqi immigrant living in Phoenix, Arizona, ran over his 20-year-old daughter, Noor, with his Jeep. She was becoming too "westernized," he told the police, and brought him dishonor by leaving an arranged marriage to an older cousin in Iraq. She died in the hospital two weeks later. In 2011 the father was sentenced to 34 years in prison.

Munira told the congregation how she was locked in her room and was praying to Jesus for strength while pushing herself toward the window an inch at a time to be careful not to fall from the chair. She described how, once reaching the window, she cut the ropes against the windowsill edge, her hands turning into a bloody mess. After several hours she was able to free herself and escape through the window to the neighboring village where the American missionaries were staying.

They brought Munira that same morning to the American Embassy in Dushanbe where she was issued a U.S. visa while being a guest of the Embassy. Munira came to Minnesota where she was enrolled at Bethany

Missionary College in Bloomington, Minnesota (now renamed Bethany Global University). After graduation she decided to go back to her native country to witness to the people walking in the darkness of Islam.

I wrote a personal letter to Munira's father, a colonel, and gave it to her as she was about to leave. In my letter I told Munira's father, Mirniyaz, that I came from a military background, my dad being a colonel and I being a first lieutenant in reserves. I told the colonel that his daughter spoke at our Grace Slavic Evangelical Church and told us how much she loved and respected him as a father and how much she loved the rest of the family including her grandfather, the Imam. In my letter I related the story about "a certain man at Caesarea named Cornelius, a Centurion (a colonel in today's terms), of what was called the Italian cohort" (regiment of 100 soldiers strong) from Acts 10:1. The Bible says that "Cornelius was a devout man who feared God with all his household, giving many alms to the Jewish people and praying to God continually" vs.2. It was Simon Peter whom God sent 2000 years ago to witness to the centurion's family and close friends about His Son Jesus' ministry, death and glorious resurrection. The text says that Peter, being Jewish, understood, after seeing a vision from heaven, that "God is not one to show partiality, but in EVERY NATION the man who fears Him and does what is right, is WELCOME TO HIM" verses 34,35. The entire centurion's family, hearing that through Jesus, "everyone who believes in Him receives forgiveness of sins" and experiencing the "Holy Spirit (that) fell upon all those who were listening to the message" got baptized "in the name of Jesus Christ" verses 43,44,48. The centurion and his family were one of the first Gentiles who followed Jesus Christ.

I told Mirniyaz that his daughter made the right choice in her life receiving Jesus as Lord and Savior and encouraged him to do the same. I also told him that his courageous daughter Munira and our entire congregation were praying for him and for the salvation of his family. Only the Lord knows what happened to Munira upon her arrival home since I lost track of her.

The teachers of Islam say it is a religion of peace but this is contradicted by verses from the Koran that suggest violence toward non-Muslims. The Koran tells its followers 109 times to kill and make war on ALL nonbelievers. "Fighting is ordained for you and slay them wherever ye find them, and drive them out of the places where they drove you out, for persecution is worse than slaughter... and fight them until fitnah (affliction or distress) is no more, and religion is for Allah" Quran, Sura 2:19.

In Sura 9:5 prophet Muhammad, (570-632 a.d.) admonishes his followers, "but when the forbidden months are past, then fight and slay the pagans wherever ye find them, and seize them, beleaguer them, and lie in wait for them in every stratagem (of war)."

Compare with Jesus Christ's teachings, "a new commandment I give to you, that you love one another, even as I have loved you, that you also love one another" John 13:34. "Love your enemies, and do good, and lend, expecting nothing in return; and your reward will be great, and you will be sons of the Most High; for He himself is kind to ungrateful and evil men. Be merciful, just as your Father is merciful" Luke 6:35,36.

Chapter 10   SLAVIC MINISTRIES

In April of 1995 we filed Articles of Incorporation for Slavic Ministries, the specific primary purpose of which was to provide spiritual, educational and humanitarian relief to the people of Ukraine. Along with Slavic Ministries Board member, Doug Peterson, his wife, Judy, and their children, we traveled to Ukraine several times to preach the Gospel and perform outreaches in a number of Ukrainian cities and villages. Doug and Judy are committed Christians as are their three children and their spouses. The family is very talented musically. Their family gospel group, "Heart Song," (www.heartsongministries.net) celebrated forty years of ministry. This group is widely known in the Midwest and beyond. The Petersons donated hundreds of Heart Song CDs and are very popular in Ukraine.

Konotop

On one of those trips, in 1993, Doug and I traveled to Konotop, a city of 95,000 people located in the northern part of Ukraine. The public transportation system of Konotop has trams which is very unusual for a city with such a relatively small population. But this is because the city is the home of a large tram factory There is a legend about the name of the city "Konotop" saying that when the Tatar cavalry was moving through the region many people and horses drowned in the swamps. So the area was named Konotop, which means swampy land where horses drowned.

The local brothers organized an outreach at the city's Palace of Culture. The mini bus picked us up at our hotel and we were on our way. Halfway to the Palace the driver picked up three shady looking hitchhikers in their late twenties. Doug and I looked at each other and started praying. We had money donated to us by Christians in Minnesota for Ukrainian churches. We carried the money with us at all times, not trusting the hotel personnel. The Lord prompted us to witness to the hitchhikers telling them that we were missionaries who came to their city to tell them about the love of Jesus. They listened attentively and we safely made it to our final destination. Brothers later told us that the mafia works together with bus drivers who tip them off about passengers to target. It was a close call that afternoon but Jesus saw us through.

Doug and I shared our testimonies and invited people to pray. There was a small group of local Christians in the audience. An old gray-haired man stood on his knees and fervently prayed for the salvation of his city, thanking the Lord for sending us from far away America to share the Gospel. He said that he had been praying for that moment for years and we were the first missionaries to come to Konotop. People had tears in their eyes as we thanked the Almighty God for his leading. Doug and I will always remember that trip to Konotop.

Crimea

In 1999 Doug and I were invited to Crimea along with Oksana Polischuk, a well known singer from California. We brought our own sound equipment and guitars that Doug later donated to the local church. A few hours before our concert our tour bus was broken into and all the equipment and instruments were stolen. The brethren called the local police and they were able to locate the thieves who had climbed over a hill with our equipment, trying to hide it in the bushes. They seemingly ran out of steam because the equipment was very heavy and the police easily apprehended them with the goods. The main culprit's name was Mikhail Romanov (I still remember his face and the famous Romanov last name). Local television crews came to interview us. Our story was broadcast over the entire Crimean peninsula. We unhinderedly shared Jesus. The interviewer was amazed that Doug did not want to press charges, but it gave us the opportunity to talk about forgiveness. "For if you forgive men for their transgressions, your heavenly Father will also forgive you" Matthew 6:14. The Lord works in mysterious ways.

Lviv

In 1994 I organized a missionary concert tour in western Ukraine with Crossroads Evangelical Church choir from Forest Lake, Minnesota. After visiting several cities and villages in that beautiful part of Ukraine surrounded by the majestic Carpathian mountains, we arrived in the city of Lviv which is famous for its unique Opera house built in 1900. We went to the central Freedom Square where the Opera house is situated to perform with our group of about thirty people. We had rehearsed several Ukrainian Christian songs including the Ukrainian National Anthem and the sacred hymn which starts with the words, "Great and powerful God

Almighty keep our Ukraine safe." As hundreds of people started gathering in the square we noticed that several police squad cars surrounded the square. We were confronted by the police chief who angrily asked me, "who are you and who allowed you to come here?" I spoke with him in Ukrainian explaining that we were from the United States and wanted to share the "Good News" with the Ukrainian people for whom we'd been praying for years. I also told him that the great Ukrainian poet, Taras Shevchenko (1814-1861) wrote in the poem "Dream" that we will yet wait for our Washington with new and righteous law" (*ми ще дочекаємося Вашінгтону з новим і праведним законом*). Shevchenko dreamed of the time when Ukraine would have it's own Washington. He was a major figure of the Ukrainian national revival and whose literary heritage is regarded to be the foundation of modern Ukrainian literature.

The police chief was awestruck and responded to the other officers by saying, these are our people! (*це ж наші люди)!* We performed Ukrainian songs, several of which we repeated twice at the request of the police chief who ordered the rest of the police officers to stay to the end and protect, in his words, "our dearest American friends." We shared our testimonies and prayed with people who were seemingly moved. At the end, the chief sincerely thanked us for coming and gave me a big bear hug that lasted for a while. It was the Lord God Almighty Who gave us liking in the chief's sight just like He once gave favor to Jacob in the sight of Esau (Genesis 33:8). Glory to God.

In 1995 there was another trip to Lviv and western Ukraine with Doug Peterson (we have traveled together to Ukraine seven times) and Galina Gabrielle, a well-known Ukrainian American singer and composer who grew up in western Ukraine.

Galina Gabrielle

On that tour we were joined by my good friends, Oleksandr Vasylenko, People's Artist of Ukraine, and my coordinator for Slavic Ministries in Ukraine, Vladimir Zybin.

Oleksandr Vasylenko and Vladimir Zybin

We performed in palaces of culture and a local juvenile prison where Galina emotionally appealed to young inmates not to lose hope but to put their trust in Jesus. "He will see you through, repent and receive Him in your hearts - He is your true Freedom!" were her words. Apostle Paul, writing to the church in Galatia, said "For you were called to freedom, brethren; only do not turn your freedom into an opportunity for the flesh, but through love serve one another." Galatians 5:13.

This trip turned out to be quite an adventure when we made a side trip to visit Galina's relatives in the village where Galina grew up. We were traveling in a mini van with a very inexperienced driver who, unbeknownst to us, had just received a driver's license. When he sideswiped a bus and lost his side mirror, he didn't skip a beat but continued driving as if nothing had happened. We could have been killed several times, including an incident on a dark night on a narrow road when the van nearly plunged into a deep canal. As we were approaching our destination to see Galina's adopted mother and grandmother, the van got stuck in the mud. When we tried to push the van, the driver accelerated which resulted in spinning wheels covering us in mud from head to toe. This adventure to that particular village greatly increased our prayer life. Thank you, Lord Jesus, for protecting us.

Train To Zhitomir

On one of my trips to Ukraine I met the leader of the Evangelical Baptist Youth, Pavlo Hrapak. I remember his testimony how he came to Christ through tremendous adversity. He had a motorcycle accident and the doctors wanted to amputate his leg. He pleaded with the Lord to save his life and promised to serve Him for the rest of his life. The Lord miraculously healed him and Pavlo kept his promise. He rededicated his life to Christ and became a youth pastor and, eventually, the senior pastor of First Baptist Church of Zhitomir.

In the late 1990s Pavlo and I traveled together by train from Kyiv to Zhitomir where I was scheduled to speak at the youth rally. All the train tickets were sold out but we were fortunate enough to get on that train since one more car was added to the train to accommodate additional passengers. We were in the last train car with thirty other passengers. A couple hours into our trip, at about ten o'clock in the evening, a scruffy looking guy passed through our car looking at peoples' belongings. Evidently my American suitcase caught his eye and he attempted to steal it at which point the train conductor, a muscular Ukrainian lady, started yelling at him and asked him to leave our car. The last words that I heard from him were "don't push me around, I've worked on trains for many years." He went back to his own car, we thought. We noticed, however, that the train seemed to be slowing down. Actually, only our car had slowed down because he had disconnected it from the rest of the train that continued on it's way not realizing that our car had been left behind in the middle of nowhere. Panic ensued! All the passengers were afraid to stay in the car for fear of another oncoming train crashing into us. The alternative was to disembark into the cold dark night. We urged people to stay in the car. Then Pavlo and I raised our voices and asked everyone to quiet down for a prayer. You could hear a pin drop. We asked the Lord to save our lives and send help. We also offered the salvation prayer to those poor frightened souls to make sure they would know the promise of eternal life. After about an agonizing hour we felt a strong jolt. It was our train that returned to pick us up. Somehow the train engineer realized what had happened. MInd you, our car conductor had no means of communicating our dire situation to the engineer driving the train. It truly was a miracle that we were rescued. It was a remarkable answer to prayer. People rushed to us hugging and kissing us, thanking us for encouraging them and offering hope in Jesus.

This reminds me of a remarkable story of a shipwreck in the book of Acts, how Apostle Paul, who encountered the angel of God, encouraged the sailors to stay on the ship and thus all 276 persons were saved. Acts 27:37.

Abkhazia

In 2006 I was invited by Eugene Bardosh, evangelical Baptist youth leader in Sacramento, to visit Abkhazia, a break-away region of the former Soviet Republic Georgia. The trip included a visit to a local Baptist church in Sukhumi where local brethren did not see eye to eye. There was ethnic feuding and outright war between the Abkhazians and Georgians since Abkhazians wanted to be an autonomous country.

Russian troops took advantage of the situation, siding with Abkhazia which had declared independence from Georgia in 1999. Russians occupied the country and have remained in control since 2008.

Our mission was to encourage the feuding church congregation and bring peace. We flew from Sacramento to Moscow and then to Adler/Sochi airport as our final destination. Our flight from Moscow was delayed four hours so we arrived at the Adler/Sochi airport very late at night.

I was the first to go through passport control with my American passport at Russian controlled Adler. The next passport control was at the Abkhazian checkpoint across the bridge. When I showed my American passport the Abkhazian customs officer looked at me disapprovingly and suspiciously (the American government supported the Georgians in the conflict). My travel companion (with his Russian passport) passed right through customs to cross the border. I, on the other hand, was taken to another area. After a delay, a guard was called to escort me. With his AK-47 on his right shoulder he led me down a path through a dark forest. Not knowing what was happening, it was a very ominous and terrifying experience. I was praying for the Lord's protection. We walked without saying a word to each other for about 700 feet. My strategy was to walk close to him on the side where he had the machine gun so that in case he would attempt to shoot me I would be able to grab his gun and trip him. Luckily (this is the wrong word) under Christ's protection, it didn't happen and we arrived at a well camouflaged hut.

When the guard opened the door I saw a young major sitting on a couch watching... American cartoons on a fuzzy screen! The tv reception was really bad--Bugs Bunny was barely recognizable. I tried to hide my laughter as the Abkhazian cartoon fan was asking me immigration questions seemingly upset that I was interrupting his show. I told him that I was an American missionary, and invited him to come to church where I would be speaking. He came twice! Eugene, who had a Russian passport and cleared the customs checkpoint in no time, was anxiously waiting and praying for me at the other side of the bridge. Thank you Jesus for the answered prayer, I needed it.

Doctor, Where Is My Leg?

I would like to relate another interesting experience that happened in 2004. A casual acquaintance, Valeriy Chernyavskiy, whom I hadn't seen in over 30 years, called me at our house in Minnesota asking me for a leg prosthesis. I was quite surprised to hear from him and told him that I was planning to come to

Kyiv In a few months and would be glad to see him and assess the situation. Approximately three months after our conversation I arrived in Kyiv with my friend and brother in Christ, Bob Jacks, from Connecticut. I called Valeriy to arrange a meeting with him while Bob decided to stay in the room. We were staying at the House of the Gospel Central Church dormitory. It was early winter and the first snow had just fallen.. Valeriy and his wife Natasha welcomed me at their beautifully renovated apartment not too far from downtown. I was surprised to see such luxury and asked Valeriy what he was doing for a living. Here is his story.

A year or so before, he was watching television late at night. All of a sudden he felt a piercing pain in his right leg. His leg was very swollen and started to turn black from the toes all the way up. The ambulance was called and he was taken to the hospital. The doctor said that Valeriy had a blood clot which could cause his death. Valeriy was anesthetized and vaguely remembers hearing the sound of an electric saw as the surgeon was amputating his leg above the knee to save his life. Valeriy was fifty three at the time.

As Valeriy was telling me his story there was a knock at the door and two men in their twenties, whose appearance was quite menacing, walked into the room. One wanted to talk to Valeriy but was hesitant because of me. I was dressed in a suit and a tie which may have led them to assume that I was "the boss". Valeriy ordered them to sit down and start speaking. The older of the two said, "we took care of the woman, we knocked her down and she hit her head real hard. Now what shall we do with her husband?" I instinctively said, "don't do anything to him, leave him alone!" The two hoods thought I was calling the shots and Valeriy grinned and told them not to do anything yet.

As they proceeded to the door I asked Valeriy, now for the second time, what exactly was he doing for a living !?! As it turned out Valeriy and his buddy, Senya Kostovetskiy, controlled the crime scene in Kyiv at that time. Valeriy proceeded to tell me that the doctor who operated on him was young and did not know what he was doing. "He could have saved my leg without cutting it off" he said. That didn't seem plausible because if it were not for that emergency surgery Valeriy would have died as the clot traveled up his leg. Then he told me that he wanted to kill the doctor. The two hitmen who had just "tripped the lady" and were asking what to do with her husband were, in fact, dealing with Valeriy's doctor and his wife. I pleaded with Valeriy not to kill the doctor telling him that he obviously saved his life. Valeriy was adamant and insisted that the poor doctor should pay the price. He then asked me what I would have done in his case. Would I forgive? I told him that since Jesus forgave me I would have forgiven this young doctor with a wife and two young children, especially since he had done everything he could to save Valeriy's life.

The next day, on Sunday, Bob and I were supposed to speak at the House of the Gospel Central Church and I invited Valeriy to join me there. He came with his girlfriend (!) and his driver who parked Valeriy's shiny black Mercedes right in front of the church. People at the church wondered who could that one-legged man possibly be. That morning I preached on the resurrection of Jesus and forgiveness of sins from Acts 13:16 - 41. Verse 30 said that God raised His Son from the dead and Verses 38 and 39 were   talking about forgiveness, "Therefore let it be known to you, Brethren, that through Him forgiveness of sins is proclaimed to you and through Him everyone who believes is freed from all things from which you could not be freed through the law of Moses" (Valeriy is half Jewish). As I was preaching I looked at

Valeriy   and his girlfriend and saw that she was crying whereas his face was motionless. The driver went out to smoke. When I gave an invitation to come forward to receive Jesus the girlfriend hesitantly stood up and wanted to come forward. At that moment Valeriy yanked her hand and ordered her to sit down. Bob and I tried to witness to Valeriy after the service but his heart was far from the Truth.   Satan had a firm grip on that ruthless man.

Valeriy asked me to go with him to visit his buddy, Senya, after the church service. It was getting dark and Bob decided to stay in the room. Brothers at the church prayed for me as I was getting ready for another adventure. This time I was going to the Lukyanovskaya High Security Prison where Senya was serving fifteen years for murder--his second murder.

While we were driving in the car, Valeriy told me the story of how Senya was playing cards with a Georgian merchant who came to Kyiv to sell oranges and how the Georgian was trying to cheat Senya by marking the cards. When Senya, at the age of 14, saw this he took out his knife and stuck it into the cheater's heart without saying a word. The Georgian died on the spot and Senya, being a minor at the time, was sentenced to eight years in prison without parole. The second murder was identical to the first except that Senya was already twenty-two and fast becoming the criminal authority in town *"вор в законе"*--Thief in the law. He was recognized in prison for his ruthlessness. This time Senya warned the unfortunate card player who happened to be another Georgian merchant, that he would kill him like he did the first one if he tried to cheat him. The guy thought Senya was bluffing.   It was a quick jab to the heart with a hunter's knife and another instant death. Senya was supposed to be sentenced to twenty-five years in prison without parole but got fifteen years since the judge was bribed.

I listened to all this while driving in the car with Valeriy and his friend, Alik Simonov, and, needless to say, I was "praying without ceasing." We finally arrived at the prison gate and I was getting ready to show my ID, that is my American passport. Valeriy told the guard that I was "the priest" visiting Senya and no ID was needed. Everybody knew and, should I say, feared Senya for his unpredictable violent behavior. Valeriy told me that a month earlier he had brought a famous Russian-Jewish immigrant singer from the U.S, Shafutinskiy, to Senya's prison cell "to cheer him up." We were escorted to Senya's prison cell by the guard who closed the door behind us saying "you are on your own now." Those are the times when Psalm 23 becomes near and dear to your heart, "Even though I walk through the valley of the shadow of death, I fear no evil; for Thou art with me; Thy rod and Thy staff, they comfort me" verse 4.

Senya was dressed in an Adidas sports suit (not in prison garb like everyone else) and was lying on the bed facing the wall. On the little stand nearby were fruit juices and crackers (again, not customary for inmates). When Valeriy told Senya that I was "a priest" he turned around and looked at me with surprise. "A priest?" he said. Now you should imagine his face, not very friendly since he was half asleep. I shared my testimony with him and told him that there is hope in Yeshua Jesus (Senya is Jewish). I explained that there is forgiveness that is ours to claim when we repent of our sins and receive the Son of God, the King of the Jews, as our personal Lord and Savior.

I also told Senya about the two criminals who were crucified with Jesus and how one was hurling abuses at Jesus saying, " Are You not the Christ? Save Yourself and us!" and how the other one rebuked him saying, "Do you not even fear God, since you are under the same sentence of condemnation?" The second thief sincerely asked Christ to remember him when He comes into His kingdom! Jesus answered him by saying, "Truly I say to you, today you shall be with Me in Paradise" Luke 23:39-43. I offered to pray with Senya.. He was seamingly moved. When we held hands his hands were pulsating.

I should mention that when I was visiting Senya's cell Valeriy told me how the prison guard brought Senya a pack of American cigarettes and how he reached for them and slipped and fell on his back on the cement floor that was freshly washed. He was partially paralyzed when I talked to him. When I prayed with Senya I asked the Lord Jesus to reveal Himself to him and heal him so that Senya could share his newly found faith with other criminals and be able to walk.

Psalm 103:3 says that the Lord God "pardons all our iniquities and heals all our diseases."

Senya's prison cell (Senya on right) with Valeriy (center)

When I returned to Kyiv a few months later I called Senya's wife to see how he was doing. She knew

169

who I was and told me that Senya was released due to amnesty (in fact Valeriy bribed the judges and Senya was released 5 years ahead of time as I found out later) AND that his lower back was back to normal. "Senya is at the train station now meeting a friend," she said. With a loud PRAISE THE LORD I confirmed that Jehovah Rapha, God the Healer, restored Senya's health. To God be the Glory!

You ask me what about Valeriy? Shortly after I left, Valeriy's wife called me in tears and pleaded that I should contact the United Nations and every possible organization that cares for invalids like her husband because he was "unjustly accused of first degree murder." She continued by saying, "so what they found a fur coat in our apartment belonging to...the DOCTOR'S WIFE! That doesn't prove anything. Valeriy did not kill anybody!" Natasha did not realize what she was saying and kept repeating herself that her husband was not guilty of murder. I later found out that the doctor who saved Valeriy's life was killed by Valeriy's hoodlums.

Kyiv's Festival Of Hope With Franklin Graham

At the end of 2006 I was approached by Victor Hamm's coordinating committee (Victor Hamm is a Vice-President for Billy Graham Evangelistic Association). I was interviewed by Victor Hamm for the position of alternate interpreter for Franklin Graham. It was an honor to participate in the Franklin Graham Festival of Hope in my native Kyiv July 6-8, 2007. One blustery afternoon Franklin humorously commented, "Victor, if my interpreter will be blown off the stage, get ready to substitute."

I had the privilege to speak and encourage the Festival staff in preparation for that historic event. I also was in charge of VIP sectors of the Olympic Stadium, the home of Football Club Dynamo Kyiv for which I once played. The stadium is one of the largest in Europe with a 100,000 seat capacity. Several days before the event, a Ukrainian Army colonel came to our stadium office to see if there were invitations for the Festival. He told me that he wanted to invite his soldiers to hear Franklin speak. It was a pleasant surprise for all of us. I told him that my father was a colonel and that I was a former first lieutenant. We gave him a stack of printed invitations, praying that our invitations would be put to good use. We told Franklin about the colonel and the potential of having Ukrainian soldiers at the stadium. The first day of the Festival of Hope two companies of Ukrainian military personnel came to the event. They sat near the stage in the upper rows of the stadium sector. The proud colonel sitting next to me at the VIP sector said, "my boys need to hear about God."

Franklin warmly greeted the Kyivites and then turned his attention to the soldiers asking them to stand to be recognized by the audience. It was a great start of the Festival as people cheered and applauded the courageous Armed Forces of the newly independent, sovereign, democratic Ukraine.

The program before Franklin's message featured a host of prominent Ukrainian, Russian, Belarusian and Moldovan artists, singers, musicians and world renowned athletes. The program included the massive Festival Choir of more than 3,000 singers led by choir director Sergei Yandola; the Kyiv Military Orchestra Band; and my friend, Oleksandr Vasylenko, People's Artist of Ukraine (we had traveled together previously with concerts in Ukraine, Minneapolis and Sacramento). Additional participants included my friend and brother in Christ Stephan Reshko of Ukraine's 1976 Olympic soccer team; Oleg Maskaev, a world WBC heavyweight boxing champion (and committed Christian whom I knew from our meetings at New Life Evangelical Baptist Church in Hollywood, Florida); Boris Uvarov, world champion speed skater and others.

On the first night of the Festival of Hope Franklin Graham preached about Nicodemus from John 3. The majority of 41 million Ukrainians are, by and large, religious. Yet, their knowledge of Jesus Christ, the Son of God, Himself being God in flesh and the soon coming Messiah, is superficial at best. People have a vestige of traditional religion, yet have not experienced a personal relationship with Jesus as personal Lord and Savior. The Bible teaches that personal knowledge of our Redeemer comes through faith in Christ's sacrificial death on the cross. Franklin told the press that he didn't come to "preach religion" but rather point Ukrainians to a personal relationship with Jesus Christ. He started by quoting Jesus saying, "I am the way, and the truth, and the life; no one comes to the Father, but by Me" John 14:6.

Franklin explained the difference between scholastic religion that the Pharisee Nicodemus personified, that is mere belief in God, and a personal relationship with Christ through repentance and born again experience. "Unless one is born again, he can not see the kingdom of God," Franklin quoted John 3:3 and "you must be born again" John 3:7. He was explaining the Scriptures and the meaning of the wind which blows where it wishes so that one could hear the sound of it but not know where it is going, so is everyone who is born of the Holy Spirit. At that moment the rush of a mighty wind blew across the platform where Franklin was standing and across the stadium. You could hear the gasp of the public as they saw the heavenly illustration of the power of God's Spirit that night at the stadium.

The prayers of thousands of believers all over Ukraine and Christians in America were answered as 124,000 people came to Kyiv Olympic Stadium to hear the saving message of hope in Jesus and another 107,000 watched on satellite TV. Approximately 3,600 Ukrainians came forward to receive Christ for the first time during the Festival of Hope. To God be the glory, great things He has done!

As a side note, Franklin Graham, who buried his beloved mother Ruth on June 14th, 2007, just three weeks before the Festival of Hope in Kyiv, did not cancel the event but remained faithful to his commitment as an evangelist and crossed the ocean to tell my former compatriots, Ukrainians, that Jesus loves them and has a plan for their lives. I personally will never forget how Franklin talked about his faithful devout mother, the wife of his father, world famous evangelist, Billy Graham, for over 63 years. "Even though my mom's grave is in North Carolina, she is not there, her eternal spirit is with us. She is alive!" Indeed, "For our citizenship is in heaven, from which also we eagerly wait for a Savior, the Lord Jesus Christ; Who will transform the body of our humble state into conformity with the body of His glory, by the exertion of the power that he has even to subject all things to Himself" Philippians 3:20,21.

Franklin Graham's Tour In Boca Raton, Florida

The last time Lilli and I saw Franklin Graham speak was on January 18, 2020 at the Sunshine State Tour in Boca Raton's Sunset Cove Amphitheater in Florida. He stated his belief that our nation is at a crossroads. I couldn't agree more. This coming election will determine whether our American way of life will be altered to the point of no return. Currently our country is under a very well programmed and intentionally executed insurrectionist attack by the socialist progressives designed to intimidate and subdue America to a globalist agenda that, in the final analysis, will collapse and destroy everything that was so miraculously created and preserved since 1776. What is happening in Democrat controlled cities of this nation is pure evil condoned by the leftist liberals.

President Lincoln once said "We have been the recipients of the choicest bounties of heaven; we have been preserved these many years in peace and prosperity; we have grown in number, wealth, and powers as no other nation has ever grown. But we have forgotten God! Intoxicated with unbroken success, we have become too self-sufficient to feel the necessity of redeeming and preserving grace, too proud to pray to the God Who made us." What prophetic words.

Chapter 11 POLITICS

54th National Prayer Breakfast In Washington,D.C.

In 2005 I was invited to attend the 54th National Prayer Breakfast in our capital as part of a seventeen member delegation from Minnesota. It was Bobby Williams' doing for which I am very thankful. The event took place February 2, 2006 at the Hilton Washington. It was such an honor to be able to hear President George Bush addressing the distinguished guests from all around the world. In his words, "It is fitting we have a National Prayer Breakfast, because our nation is a nation of prayer... We are a nation founded by men and women who came to these shores seeking to worship the Almighty freely. From these prayerful beginnings, God has greatly blessed the American people, and through our prayers, we give thanks to the true source of our blessings." I remember sitting at the table with our delegation being so proud and blessed to be an American. Our table was not too far from the main podium, and I could catch every word trying to remember and write down what had been said. Irish rock musician/songwriter, Bono, of U2 talked about the importance of Christian faith in his life. Along with his wife, Alison, he traveled to Ethiopia with World Vision, an evangelical Christian humanitarian organization, to work in the camp, feeding the hungry.

I also remember the speech given by the former Pakistani Prime Minister, Benazir Bhutto, the first woman to head a democratic government in a Muslim majority nation. With genuine sincerity she spoke about the importance of prayer and the "redeeming influence of Christianity in today's world." We, at the table, looked at each other thinking that Benazir might be a secret follower of Christ. Bobby and I sensed it in our spirits since she sounded like a born again believer. I remember her burning eyes and her facial expression as she spoke about the love of God and her desire for "Christians, Jews and Muslims to live in peace in my country." At the end she thanked the President and the American people for being "the beacon of hope in this world." It was one of the highlights to hear that courageous woman sharing her heart that memorable morning in Washington. Some believe that her speech at the National Prayer Breakfast cost her her life. Tragically, at the age of 54, on December 27, 2007, two months after Benazir returned to her country after being exiled (she lived in England), she was cowardly assassinated by Muslim extremists in Rawalpindi, Pakistan along with 23 other people. She was a sincere soul and a strikingly beautiful woman.

Unapologetically Not Politically Correct

When House Democrats omitted "so help me God" during the swearing-in procedure, Steve Cohen, Democrat from Tennessee who is the Chairman of the Judiciary Committee's Subcommittee on the Constitution, Civil Rights and Civil Liberties, said "I think God belongs in religious institutions, in temple, in church, in cathedral, in mosque, but not in Congress." That was the same Steve Cohen who, during his interview with CNN during the ill construed impeachment procedure of President Trump, said with utter confidence, "we shall prevail, mark my words, we shall prevail." Trump is still in the White House and he is still our President. What Cohen and his accusers-in-arms did was a shameful waste of over 34 million of American taxpayers' hard earned dollars.

Democrats on the House Natural Resources Committee proposed a draft rule omitting "so help me God." Jerrold Nadler, Chairman of the House Judiciary Committee, was questioned by Republican Congressman Mike Johnson from Louisiana as to why Nadler swore in three witnesses omitting the phrase "so help me God." To which Nadler arrogantly replied, "We do not have religious tests for office or for anything else!"

President George Washington added the words "so help me God" during his first inaugural address April 30, 1789 to Article II, Section One, Clause 8 of the United States Constitution. It has been an American historic tradition for 231 years.

Politically, Democrats are also laying themselves open to charges that they are a godless party. In many conversations with Democrats after hearing that they are "not religious" I try to explain that faith in God is not intellectual suicide and that the soon coming Messiah Jesus is an historic figure and Himself God in flesh. It is no wonder that at the recent Democrat National

Convention the words "one nation under God" were omitted deliberately twice from the Pledge of Allegiance by two Convention speakers, a Muslim cleric and gay activist.

The words of Franklin Graham warn of the moral collapse of America, "In my mind the year 2020 will mark a defining watershed year in the long and storied history of our great nation. Will we continue to protect the freedoms of Christians to live and abide by their Biblical convictions? Will pastors be able to proclaim and preach the uncompromising Word of God without their messages labeled as "hate speech?" Will the sexual agenda of the LGBTQ lobby be forced on our schools and children? I believe our nation is perched on a sheer moral precipice. If we are undermined much more by the decadent values of the leftist-progressives, we could plunge into a perilous moral collapse."

Apostle Paul wrote in his second letter to Timothy, "But realize this, that in the last days difficult times will come.

For men will be lovers of self, lovers of money, boastful, arrogant, revilers, disobedient to parents, ungrateful, unholy, unloving, irreconcilable, malicious gossips, without self-control, brutal, haters of good, treacherous, reckless, conceited, lovers of pleasure rather than lovers of God" 2 Timothy 3:1-4.

Judeo-Christian values are at the very root of America's democracy and success. Yet this notion is flatly denied by the Democrat Socialists of America (DSA). Here is what its National Director, Maria Svart, devout follower of Bernie Sanders, recently said, "We have to fundamentally transform America and take over the institutions." This is exactly what Bolsheviks did in 1917 in Russia. Check out the words to the International Communist Anthem on the site marxists.org. That was the communists' play book back then and the socialist democrats' agenda today. Lenin and his ruthless mob followed the lyrics of the Anthem to the T: "arise ye prisoners of want, for reason of revolt now thunders...away with all your superstitions...we'll change henceforth the old tradition and spurn the dust to win the prize...no more deluded by reaction on tyrants only we'll make war...and if those cannibals keep trying to sacrifice us to their pride, they soon shall hear the bullets flying, we'll shoot the generals on our own side...no savior from on high delivers (Russian lyrics: 'neither God, nor tsar, nor hero'--English translation: 'no faith have we in prince or peer') our own right hand the chains must shiver, chains of hatred, greed and fear, e'er the thieves will out with their booty, and give to all a happier lot, each at the forge must do their duty, and we'll strike while the iron is hot."

Svart goes on: "I believe in freedom of speech, but it should be shut down." The Democrat Socialists of America (DSA) is not alone. One of two openly Marxist groups is Antifa (far-left militant anarchists who use the symbols of the red flag of the 1917 Russian revolution and the black flag of 19th century anarchists). This group is involved in major vandalism, using improvised explosive devices and other homemade weapons. They are unashamedly proclaiming Marxist slogans. The Biden-Harris duo does not even conceal their ties with Antifa. Recently, when looking up www.antifa.com I was re-addressed directly to www.biden.com. The photo of Biden-Harris was accompanied by the phrase "Together we will beat Trump" coupled with a request for money. Nothing about America and Americans, just zeroing in on Trump and how to get rid of him.

The second radical group is Black Lives Matter. It is a corporation whose real name is Black Lives Matter Global Network Foundation (BLMGNF). It is a nationwide corporation with chapters in Boston, Chicago,

Washington D.C., Denver, Detroit, Los Angeles, Lansing, Long Beach, Memphis, Nashville, New York City, Philadelphia, South Bend and in Canada in Toronto, Vancouver, and Waterloo. So if you were impressed by how all the recent riots erupted simultaneously from a "grassroots movement" well...maybe it was not so "grassroots." Black lives do matter just as EVERY life matters. Two thousand years ago Jesus Christ ended the debate on which lives matter. He died on the cross of Calvary FOR ALL. Currently the BLM movement personifies riots, looting, and destruction.

BLM was founded by radical Marxists (by their own admission) Patrisse Cullors, who said "we are trained Marxists;" Alicia Garza, a Black woman; and Opal Tometi, transnational feminist, who advocate for civil unrest and violence. BLM is a toxic fraudulent organization which together with Antifa has been terrorizing downtowns of Democrat controlled American cities while their mayors looked on. The Left is encouraging the destruction of American cities with their politicization of black tragedy.

California BLM leader, 20-year old Tianna Arata, who is charged with five felonies, said recently that "BLM will be going to suburbs so that they might feel our pain."

On May 31, 2020 President Trump announced that he intended to designate Antifa as a terrorist organization. Attorney General William Barr similarly remarked that "violence instigated and carried out by Antifa and other similar groups in connection with the rioting is domestic terrorism and will be treated accordingly."

After the tragic death of Black American, George Floyd, in Minneapolis May 25th, 2020 these two and other militant groups organized civil protests in 140 American cities. More than 1,500 small businesses were destroyed and streets in Minneapolis were set ablaze (and they call it "peaceful protests")? Doctor Martin Luther King did not march at night. "Peaceful demonstrations" ceased being "peaceful" at dusk when looting and vandalism began. And now there is a movement in Democrat controlled cities to defund and "restructure" the police force! Really? Anarchists fully understand that the local police is the last line of defense. Abolish police and all hell will break loose.

I just read an article on Facebook called AND IN 1933…"In 1933 Hitler appointed Hermann Göring Minister of the Interior. His first orders were to defund and eliminate police departments so that they would not interfere with his Brown Shirts whose mission it was to riot, burn, beat up and kill citizens in an effort to sway the elections."

In August, 2015 "peaceful protesters" of the BLM movement marched in Minneapolis, blocking streets and highways chanting "pigs in a blanket (referring to police) fry'em like bacon." It was then that hate crimes abounded in Minneapolis and Saint Paul and the local liberal press kept mum about it. Lawlessness in the downtown area was running rampant. For me it hits close to home. My oldest son, a father of two small children, was walking to his car parked in a lot in downtown Minneapolis, a block away from the police precinct. He was attacked by three black men for no reason. They kicked him down to the ground and started beating him despite my son's plea for mercy crying out that he had two small kids at home. He also said it must be a case of mistaken identity. The barbarians did not say a word and continued kicking his body and head. His face was a bloody mess at that point. The attackers were beating him to kill because when my son was not moving (our son told us that he was praying to Jesus to spare his life) one of the attackers snapped, "he is done, let's go." We saw our son's disfigured face the next day…We are thankful that the Lord protected him so he could return to his precious family.

Fast forward to present day. It boggles my mind and defies human reasoning to see how present day left wing savages destroy their own communities, topple historic monuments, attempting to cause utter destruction of property and the American way of life. American history is being obliterated by the radical left wing vandals. For the longest time neither Biden nor his running mate, Senator Kamala Harris, condemned the violence. In fact Harris remarked on September first on the Stephen Colbert show that "protests will not stop and should not stop--not even after election day, we should be sure of that."

During a September 15th virtual roundtable discussion Kamala Harris "accidentally" announced plans for the "Harris administration together with Joe Biden." While speaking in Tampa, Biden, on the same day, reading from a teleprompter, said, "a Harris-Biden administration is going to relaunch that effort (appealing to veterans)." Is there any doubt who Democrats are grooming for the presidential seat?

Talking about the left, I like this verse from the Bible. "A wise man's heart directs him toward the right, but the foolish man's heart directs him toward the left" Ecclesiastes 10:2. Quite succinct, simple and to the point.

Nowadays, Democrats are doing everything possible to discredit President Trump and his cabinet before the elections November 3rd. We had our fair share of Russia-gate and then Ukraine-gate. It was a shameful and costly impeachment circus. Democrats are turning Congress into an "impeachment machine" at taxpayers' expense.

Accusations by Biden and his "election team" (the liberal press) that President Trump mismanaged the

COVID-19 crises calling him "downright un-American for not acting earlier and concealing the truth about the virus" are hypocritical. Our President did the right thing keeping the country calm, avoiding panic and a run on banks and groceries. Never mind that he announced a ban on China travel two weeks after the world found out, January 20, that the new COVID-19 virus was transmitted by air. The ban was enforced February 2, 2020 and the liberal press was infuriated. Never mind that Trump halted travel from Europe to the U.S. to stop the spread of coronavirus across the country. The Coronavirus Task Force was headed by Vice-President Mike Pence. It included top health officials sitting on the advisory panel formed by President Trump. Daily briefings took place updating the nation. In the meantime Biden was hiding out in his basement in Wilmington and receiving his $248,670 pension and travel funds among other benefits--all the while criticizing the President. Trump, on the other hand, faithfully continued his daily service to the country he loves, collecting a yearly salary in the amount of $1. What an irony!

Biden called Trump "xenophobic and racist" (because our president called coronavirus "the Chinese virus." Didn't it originate in Wuhan, China!? Biden said that Trump had a "record of hysteria, xenophobia, and fear-mongering." More and more critics realize that Trump did the right thing and saved hundreds of thousands of lives. Biden wrote Trump a letter of apology three months later. Joe come lately. Now his staff denies it, of course.

Meanwhile, Speaker Pelosi was visiting San Francisco's Chinatown February 24th. Amid coronavirus concerns, when Pelosi was surrounded by well wishers she encouraged them to ignore Trump and "have a party to celebrate our diversity." Yet another Trump "well wisher," Governor Cuomo, at the same time as Nancy, did not heed warnings and encouraged New Yorkers "to go out" while the coronavirus was silently spreading around the country.

The Left blames our President for riots, civil unrest, and disturbances in our country; for COVID-19 handling; for absolutely EVERYTHING under the sun. I just wonder how much more cynical could these guys get in their open hatred for the duly elected president. To give you an example, one neighbor quite seriously told me he would rather vote for Mickey Mouse than for Trump. Recently at the Lake Minnetonka boat landing a middle aged woman with her teenage daughter said a friendly "hi" to me then changed her tune when she saw my Trump-Pence 2020 bumper sticker and started shouting, "F-you and your Trump!   He is a racist anti-semite." She went on accusing Trump of being a "xenophobic and homophobic jerk," and then pointing her finger at me, her face full of rage, saying, "and so are you! F-you!" Mind you, she was a complete stranger. Then her husband came out from the car yelling the same thing. Lilli stayed in the car in shock. I guess it is a new norm for Trump haters--yelling obscenities.

Incidentally, here is Trump on anti-semitism, "the vile, hate-filled poison of anti-semitism must be condemned and confronted everywhere and anywhere it appears!" I am sorry, but those are not the words of an anti-semite. Jewish believer in Jesus, Dr. Michael L. Brown, said, "I am voting for the man who has been called "America's First Zionist President."

And regarding the issue of pro-life, not a single democrat leader is pro-life including Biden and Harris whereas President Trump is the strongest pro-lifer the White House has had in a long time. The battle over abortion on demand is much more than the right of "choice," but about an agenda to stop Christians from advocating for their most basic rights. Abortion on demand, de-facto, is the premeditated murder of our American treasure--children, not the euphemistic "removal of fetal tissue." Partial birth and late term abortion is murder no matter how pro-choice advocates address it. It is unconscionable to allow a mother and her health provider to decide whether her newly-born living breathing child lying on the table lives or dies, having his or her right to life snuffed away.

Now explain to me how one can speak about being a Christian while planning to vote for the party that does not defend a child's basic right to life, but supports public funding for abortion. I was just thinking, aren't people afraid of the wrath of God? Didn't the Giver of Life, the God of Israel, declare in His 6th Commandment: "You shall not murder" Exodus 20:13! As quoted by Franklin Graham, "When a culture rejects the truth and the authority of God, then it has rejected none other than God Himself."

I am painfully aware that some family members and friends are planning to give their votes to the Democrat Party, the party that has lost its moral compass and is totally hijacked by radical socialists. As a father and a retired pastor, I plead with you, to vote your Christian conscience for your own sake, for the sake of your children, and for the sake of the country you live in. Biden and Harris are godless people and as such will drive this country to destruction if elected.

For lifelong DFLers it should be apparent that the current Democrat Party has been hijacked by the radical Left. How many more riots, lootings and killings will it take to make one realize that the Democrat Party of today is far from being the one you embraced for years and decades. To quote Vice-President Mike Pence, dear Brother in Christ, "the truth is, the Democratic Party has been taken over by radical leftists who want higher taxes, open borders, late-term abortion, and socialist policies that would crush our economy and destroy our country." I pray to God that in your heart of hearts you agree with him. Pence is a man of integrity and strong faith. Here's a fair question: if both Trump and Biden are gone, who would you rather have for your president--Pence or Harris?

I know that the questions I posed are immaterial and meaningless to some who do not share Christian values and who do not put their trust in the Son of God, Jesus Christ, Who is still calling, "Come to Me, all who are weary and heavy laden, and I will give you rest. Take My yoke upon you, and learn from Me, for I am gentle and humble in heart; and YOU SHALL FIND REST FOR YOUR SOULS. For My yoke is easy, and My burden is light" Matthew 11:28-30.

The Bible is clear regarding the supremacy of Christ Who is the "Way, the Truth and the Life." The verse in John 14:6 continues to say "...no one comes to the Father, but through Me." "No one" means no religious leader past or present, no Muhammad, no Buddha nor Confucius is able to bring a person into the fellowship with the Mighty God of Abraham, Isaac and Jacob Who revealed Himself in His only begotten Son Jesus Christ. "He (she) who believes in Him (Jesus) is not judged; he who does not believe has been judged already, because he has not believed in the name of the only begotten Son of God." John 3:18.

"Come now, and let us reason together" Isaiah 1:18. I did not vote for a choirboy in 2016 when I voted for Donald Trump. I know that personalities often affect our decisions but what is more important is the actual delivered results. Should we trust a politician who for over 47 years didn't do much for the country or continue with the man who is blessed with the God given talent of business vision and leadership; the man, who for the past three and a half years has done so much for the country, and is still fully capable, eager and willing to further lead our ONE NATION UNDER GOD USA which I know you honor, love, and pray for.

I realize I am being brutally honest and I apologize for possibly offending some of you, but I simply cannot be politically correct at this pivotal historic time for the country of which I am a proud citizen by choice, not by birth. I am proud of our blessed country--America and its flag, the land I have called my country for the past 45 years; the land I have grown to love, cherish, be proud of, and pray for.

I lived in communist USSR for 26 years, I've been to that movie before and know full well how it ends. In my former country the government controlled all aspects of daily life including the economy with its "Five-year plans;" education, where students were brainwashed from an early age; health care with long lines and doctor's appointments that were hard to obtain unless you paid a bribe; bribes to get employment; bribes to get housing. Individuals in the former USSR had little or no freedom or decision-making ability. Political dissent was not tolerated and those who tried to voice their opinion contrary to the Party lines were persecuted. I am well aware of what communists did to their own country, my native Ukraine, and elsewhere in the world where they ventured to spread their godless influence--be it China, North Korea, Vietnam, Cambodia, former East Germany, Angola, Mozambique, Ethiopia, Cuba or recently Venezuela to name a few. I am not alone in my opinion. There are over 35,000 immigrants from the former Soviet Union living in Minnesota. I would be hard pressed to find ONE immigrant in our community, Jew or Gentile, who would not agree that today's situation in Democrat controlled cities in America reminds us of the former Soviet Union. There are no Democrat voters among our ranks that I know of. .

Decades ago Soviet communists had a well devised destructive plan to ruin the United States from within. Sadly their plan is currently being fulfilled right before our very eyes with the willing help of the radical Left wing Socialist Democrats.

In 1917 Russian bolsheviks (communists) promised the gullible university students and workers "freedom, equality and brotherhood," and then for the following 70 years terrorized the country and turned it into a mediocre, pitiful state. The Biden-Harris ticket is promising the world to our gullible millennials who, according to recent polls, prefer to live in socialist America where everything is magically "free." The Democrats are shamelessly using our current coronavirus situation to try to sell the American people their Big Government Socialist laundry list of extremely costly and unrealistic Left-wing utopian ideas. They include free government-paid college tuition for everybody; free national health care for all including over 11 million illegal aliens (their future "voting block"); open borders for all immigrants (which would be a logistical nightmare); dangerous abortion policies; allowing inmates to vote (another voting block); lowering the voting age to sixteen; supporting sanctuary cities; defunding police departments; cutbacks in US military spending. And that is when China, Russia, Iran and North Korea are the real threat to our Democracy and are building their nuclear arsenal as we speak.

The radical Left is trying to erase our nation's history; pack the Supreme Court (adding more liberal justices for the Left's ultimate control); make Washington D.C. a state where Democrats make up 76 percent of registered voters; abolish the electoral college so that the west and east coasts, which are predominantly represented by Democrats, will control the rest of the country perpetually; and, finally, introduce extreme climate change programs which by 2050 will cost $35 billion per year according to Forbes and the Wall Street Journal. Our kids and grandkids will be footing the bill.

If the socialist Left succeeds, the above mentioned "changes" will permanently alter the United States and our way of life. Our country, for which generations of Americans fought and died, will be controlled by the Big Government Socialist Democrats for decades. Millennials, don't buy this bunk! Biden (who will turn 78 November 20th) will tax everything that moves. That will include you. Remember, companies are composed of people, aka tax-payers like you. Rich people will move their assets elsewhere like they did during the Obama-Biden presidency. Biden already promised higher taxes, and plans to shut down the U.S. economy if "scientists recommend to do so." Harris will continue to wage a class war masquerading it as racial equality and social justice.

In a recent CNN interview Harris sounded off about systemic racism in the U.S. Never mind that we had a Black president for eight years, 52 Black lawmakers in the House, 51 of which are Democrats. This year at least 26 Black candidates have won primary elections in additional districts with large shares of white residents. Finally, Biden chose Harris, a woman of color, as his running mate. This is the same Biden whom Harris angrily chastised during Democrat Presidential Debates for his stance on busing and segregation. You simply cannot make it up! The convenient race card will be played by Harris long after Biden is gone if democrats win in November.

Trump Campaign Rally in Minneapolis

I signed up on line to attend the rally at the Target Center on October 10,2019 with over 100,000 others. I took a public bus from Maple Grove. Several people on the bus were headed downtown for the same event. When we arrived I saw thousands of people waiting in line. Secret Service security police were directing the traffic of people who seemed to be coming from everywhere. The energy and friendly atmosphere was contagious as people encouraged each other that we'd have a chance to get inside and see and hear our President. The big TV monitors outside featured prominent athletes, musicians and political leaders. Lara Lea Trump, a campaign adviser, was instructing people to stay cool if Antifa and BLM agitators would try to provoke the crowd.

Sure enough, groups of 30-50 people dressed in black with red bands on their sleeves and carrying anti Trump signs appeared, openly shouting obscenities at us as the city mounted police looked on. The verbal attacks lasted the entire time we were outside. Our response was "USA, USA and Trump, Trump, Trump!" Those were the unforgettable moments when I was so proud to be an American, surrounded by like minded American patriots who love their and MY country. I had the opportunity to talk with people around me about the danger of socialism-communism that the radical Left was propagating.

Target Center capacity is 19,356. While waiting in drizzling rain for three hours and praying that I would be able to be seated inside, I met a number of enthusiastic American patriots who drove from all over Minnesota to hear and support our President. That was a real grassroots event. Finally, the first come first served crowd started pouring into the Target Center. I made the cut and with a loud "thank you Jesus" joined my Republican brothers and sisters excited and energized to see, hear, and support our President. Thousands of people who were less fortunate remained outside, singing songs, cheering and encouraging each other. This is your true American spirit.

Jennifer Carnahan, the first elected Asian-American Chair for the Republican Party of Minnesota, opened up the rally with a beautiful prayer for our country and our President asking the Lord to bless our President and preserve "the land of the free and the home of the brave." The audience was moved standing up from their chairs and cheering for the USA and President Trump. Jennifer's life story is truly remarkable. She was born in South Korea in 1976 and was left on the back doorstep of a rural hospital. Five months later she was adopted by a loving family in Maple Grove, Minnesota. Jennifer lived just down the street, so our kids grew up together and went to school together. The Lord Jesus knew Jennifer and was preparing her "for such a time as this" Esther 4:14b.

President Trump acknowledged and thanked Jennifer saying, "I am proud of you Jennifer and Minnesota is proud of you." At that moment I was thinking what are the chances of a South Korean orphan girl ending up with the privilege of praying for her adopted country and the leader of the free world, only in a blessed America!

At the rally we heard from a number of people including Eric Trump and Vice-President Mike Pence who encouraged us to pray for our nation, our President, and our elected officials so that the Lord would give them wisdom from above on how to govern the country. Then Pence introduced the 45th President of the United States, Donald J.Trump. A standing ovation and chants of "USA" lasted for several minutes.

I felt deep gratitude for our Commander-in-Chief who sacrificially serves our nation and who is unjustly treated by his vicious opponents and extremely biased media. Promises made, promises kept. President Trump delivered a powerful message that evening that lasted over two hours. It was a message of hope, vision and prosperity for America by the President under whose leadership in just 3.5 years, since he was sworn in, has moved our country forward at an unprecedented pace.

America became energy independent in 2019 for the first time since 1957 when another Republican, President Dwight Eisenhower, achieved American energy independence. The largest tax cut in American history was passed; unnecessary rules and regulation instituted by the previous Obama-Biden Administration were rescinded; the military was rebuilt; our Nation's borders are being secured as we speak; our national education system is improving.

On National Religious Freedom Day, January 16, 2020, President Trump announced several new rules and memos designed to roll back "discriminatory" federal regulations as well as to promote teachers' and students' rights to pray in public schools. To that end nine agencies were instructed to draft religious freedom rules. Among them was the announcement that the U.S. Department of Education would send out memos to secretaries and administrators in all fifty states stressing that teachers or students should not be prevented from praying in public schools. The goal is to "further safeguard students' constitutionally protected right to pray in school" and to let public school administrators know that they can lose federal funding if they violate students' religious freedom. In President Trump's words, "In America we don't punish prayer, we don't ban symbols of faith, we don't muzzle preachers and pastors. In America, we celebrate faith, we cherish religion, we lift our voices in prayer and we raise our sights to the glory of God."

And, yes, right up to when COVID-19 dealt its devastating blow to our country, America's economy was performing at record levels. The economy will continue to flourish as President Trump and his Administration will have a chance to make our nation greater than it was before in the next four years. Millions of Christians around the country are praying for this.

I should mention that when the Trump rally was over and people were exiting the Target Center, Antifa and BLM agitators proved, once again, that they are not a civil rights movement but a blatant domestic terrorist organization with a definite agenda to overthrow the existing government and turn the United States into a socialist society. Rocks and bottles with urine were hurled at the unsuspecting public, cars were blocked from exiting parking lots...all of that coupled by constant obscenities and verbal threats. Protesters were beating horses of the mounted police with baseball bats causing chaos on the streets.

Days before the Trump rally the mayor of Minneapolis, 39 year old Democrat Jacob Frey, transplant from Oakton, Virginia, declared, "On October 10, our entire city will stand not behind the President, but behind the communities and people who continue to make our city and our country great." Entire city? Wait a minute, do Trump supporters like me not have a voice?

After the May 25th death of George Floyd, the irresolute mayor of Minneapolis allowed areas of the city to be looted and burned to the ground for days. Making the unprecedented decision to abandon the third police precinct downtown Minneapolis on May 28th, and allowing the violent mob to torch it was another example of wreckless city management. It exhibited an irresponsible lack of leadership by Mayor Frey who said he had decided to let the precinct burn late Thursday, May 28 after receiving reports that protesters were trying to breach the premises. "Brick and mortar is not as important as life. People had to vent their anger," Frey said in defense of the move.

When President Trump blasted "very weak" Jacob Frey on Twitter, the mayor angrily responded by saying, "Donald Trump knows nothing about the strength of Minneapolis, we are strong as hell." Interestingly, the mayor's religion does not acknowledge the existence of hell, Gehinom, Sheol, as eternal punishment for sinners. Here is a good verse for Mr. Frey to remember, "Finally, be STRONG in the LORD and in the strength of His might" Ephesians 6:10.

Global Warming

The gradual rise in the Earth's atmosphere and oceans these days is a sure sign that the Bible prophecy regarding the Second Coming of the Lord Jesus Christ is at hand. Apostle Peter, moved by the Holy Spirit, warned believers in his Second Letter that "in the last days mockers will come with their mocking, following after their own lusts and saying, "Where is the promise of His coming? For ever since the fathers fell asleep, all continues just as it was from the beginning of creation" 2 Peter 3:4. Today's radical environmentalists under the guise of "The Green New Deal" are contemplating a hit on America's energy independence in the name of science. They are those "mockers" of whom Peter was speaking. Apostle Peter goes on, "For when they maintain this, it escapes their notice that by the word of God the heavens existed long ago and the earth was formed out of water and by water through which the world at that time was destroyed, being flooded with water." Verses 5,6.

In 1982 Lilli and I, with our two children, Tania and Andrei, lived in Santa Barbara, California for three months. While there I had the privilege of attending lectures by the late Dr. Henry M. Morris (1918-2006), Christian apologist and one of the world's leading scientists. Morris was the founder of The Institute For Creation Research as well as the author of several books on scientific creationism. He opposed the billion year time scale of evolution, the age of the Earth and the age of the Universe that he saw as being contrary to it. In his book, The Genesis Flood, that he co-authored with John Whitcomb, another Christian scientist, he proves beyond the shadow of a doubt that our Planet Earth was formed "out of water and by water." Being a superb hydrologist as well as geologist, Dr. Morris used radiocarbon dating, a technique based on Carbon-14 decay, to determine the age of organic materials. He was a proponent of Young Earth Creationism (YEC) which holds as a central tenant that the Earth and its lifeforms were created in their present forms by supernatural acts of God around 10,000 years ago.

Secular opponents suggest that the age of the universe is "around 13.8 billion years," and the formation of the Earth and Solar System happened "around 4.6 billion years ago." Some scientists suggest that the hot Big Bang (mind you, not "theory" any more, but a fact in their estimation) occurred 13.8 billion years ago stating, "there is no other possible answer consistent with what we know today," and also that "there is no deity (God) that supposedly created the Earth." The words of Apostle Paul ring true today, "...they became futile in their speculations, and their foolish heart was darkened. Professing to be wise, they became fools" Romans 1:21b and 22.

These theories are taught in our schools and universities today. And then we, as parents, wonder why our children are indifferent toward God and His Word. Let me quote the rest of Peter's prophetic third chapter of 2 Peter that will give us a "hint" as to the coming apocalyptic Global warming:

"But the present heavens and earth by His word are being reserved for fire, kept for the day of judgment and destruction of ungodly men. But do not let this one fact escape your notice, beloved, that with the Lord one day is as a thousand years, and a thousand years as one day. The Lord is not slow about His promise, as some count slowness, but is patient toward you, not wishing for any to perish but for all to come to repentance. But the day of the Lord will come like a thief, in which the heavens will pass away with a roar and the elements will be destroyed with intense heat, and the earth and its works will be burned up. Since all these things are to be destroyed in this way, what sort of people ought you to be in holy conduct and godliness. Looking for and hastening the coming of the day of God, on account of which the heavens will be destroyed by burning, and the elements will melt with intense heat. But according to His promise we are looking for new heavens and a new earth, in which righteousness dwells" Verses 7-13.

The Lord seems to be warming up the Earth according to His word for the final fiery judgement of ungodly men and women and preparing new heavens and new earth for those who put their trust in Christ. "Blessed are the people whose God is the Lord" King David, Psalm 144:15b

Chapter 12   SECOND COMING OF CHRIST

Signs Of The End Times

Christians and Messianic Jews believe, and the Bible affirms, that Jesus Christ, Who is called by Prophet Isaiah "Wonderful Counselor, Mighty God, Eternal Father, Prince of Peace" Isaiah 9:6, is COMING BACK. Every prophecy of the Hebrew Bible, called Tanakh, and known to Christians as the Old Testament, regarding Jesus Christ's first coming, was fulfilled in minute detail.

The prophecy of Christ's birth in Bethlehem: "But as for you, Bethlehem Ephrathah, too little to be among the clans of Judah, from you One will go forth for Me to be ruler of Israel. His goings forth are from long ago, FROM THE DAYS OF ETERNITY" Micah 5:2.

The prophecy of the time of His birth: "So you are to know and discern that from the issuing of a decree to restore and rebuild Jerusalem until Messiah the Prince there will be seven weeks and sixty two weeks; it will be built again, with plaza and moat, even in times of distress" Daniel 9:25. (The Hebrew word for 'weeks' or 'sevens' literally means 'a unit of seven"). Thus Daniel's Seventieth Week, refers to a seven-year period that will take place at the very end of the age. In a given context this seventy week prophecy refers to seventy periods of seven years for a total of 490 years. Sixty nine of these 'weeks' of years took place between the decree given by Cyrus, king of Persia to let the exiles of Judah return and rebuild Jerusalem in 445 BC, and the arrival of Jesus Christ in Jerusalem on Palm Sunday when Jewish people were celebrating Passover, for a total of 483 years. During the final 7 year period Israel will be under the domination of an empire controlled by Satan, because when the prophesied Messiah Jesus Christ came to His own Jewish people, "those who were His own did not receive Him" John 1:11. Also: "I have come in My Father's name (Jesus speaking) and you do not receive Me; if ANOTHER (antichrist) shall come in his name, you will receive him" John 5:43. In other words, Israel rejected her true promised Messiah and Melekh - King Jesus Christ, at His First Coming.

During my pilgrimage to Israel in 1984 I saw an interesting episode while riding on a city bus in Jerusalem. A young pregnant Jewish woman was entering the bus from the front door. The bus driver was carefully helping her in. "How nice and thoughtful of him," was on my mind. She then was offered the front seat by the "Tzadik" - a respectful looking old man dressed in a long black robe who then moved to the middle of the bus. "Tzadik" means "righteous one" in Hebrew and is applied to clergy. People on the bus were looking at the young woman with some sort of special reverence and adoration. It was explained to me later that the woman "could have been pregnant with Messiah" since Jewish people expect their Messiah to come for the first time.

Prophet Zechariah, which means "Jehovah remembers," prophesied in 520 B.C., "And the Lord said to me, "Take again for yourself the equipment of FOOLISH SHEPHERD (false Messiah). "For behold, I am going to raise up a shepherd in the land who will not care for the perishing, seek the scattered, heal the broken, or sustain the one standing, but will devour the flesh of the fat sheep and tear off their hoofs. "Woe to the worthless shepherd who leaves the flock! A sword will be on his arm and on his right eye! His arm will be totally withered, and his right eye will be blind" Zechariah 11: 15-17.

Zechariah continues with more prophetic verses, God speaking: "Awake, o sword, against My Shepherd, and against the man, My Associate (Jesus Christ) declares the Lord of Hosts. Strike the Shepherd that the sheep may be scattered; (Christs' disciples were scattered when He was crucified); and I will turn My hand against the little ones (Israel). And it will come about in all the land (land of Israel), declares the Lord, that TWO PARTS IN IT WILL BE CUT OFF AND PERISH, BUT THE THIRD WILL BE LEFT IN IT. And I will bring the third part through the fire, refine them as silver is refined, and test them as gold is tested. THEY WILL CALL ON MY NAME, AND I WILL ANSWER THEM; I WILL SAY, THEY ARE MY PEOPLE, AND THEY WILL SAY, THE LORD IS MY GOD" Zechariah 13:7-9. When I witness to Jewish people I pray that the person I talk to will be in the proverbial "one third" that will be saved by faith in Jesus the Messiah. There is a remarkable verse in Zechariah 12:10 where Jesus Christ, Whose "GOINS FORTH ARE FROM LONG AGO, FROM THE DAYS OF ETERNITY," is actually speaking to His own Jewish people DIRECTLY: "And I will pour out on the house of David and on the inhabitants of Jerusalem, the Spirit of grace and of supplication, so that THEY WILL LOOK ON ME WHOM THEY HAVE PIERCED; AND THEY WILL MOURN FOR HIM, AS ONE MOURNS FOR AN ONLY SON, AND THEY WILL WEEP BITTERLY OVER HIM, LIKE THE BITTER WEEPING OVER THE FIRST-BORN."

Back To Daniel's Prophecy

So God appointed a period of time between the first 69 weeks and the 70th week that would bring the opportunity for salvation to the Goyim - Gentiles, non - Jews. Jesus said, "And I have other sheep (Gentiles), which are not of this fold (Jews); I must bring them also, and they shall hear My voice; and they shall become one flock with one shepherd" John 10:16. The Lord Jesus sent Apostle Paul to the Gentiles to reveal to them, "that the Gentiles are fellow heirs and fellow members of the body, and fellow partakers of the promise in Christ Jesus through the gospel;" "To me, the very least of the saints, this grace was given, to preach to the Gentiles the unfathomable riches of Christ, and to bring to light what is the administration of the mystery which for ages has been hidden in God, who created all things, in order that the manifold wisdom of God might now be known through the church to the rulers and the authorities in the heavenly places. This was in accordance with the eternal purpose which He carried out in Christ Jesus our Lord" Ephesians 3:6,8-11. This fulfills God's promise to Abraham, "that in you ALL the families of the earth shall be blessed" Genesis 12:3.

When Israel regained control of her land May 14,1948, and of East Jerusalem June 7, 1967, during the Six-Day War which accomplished the historic reunification of Jerusalem; and when Jerusalem, which is and always has been the geographic and spiritual center of the Jewish people for over 3,000 years, was declared to be the historic capital of the Jewish people on December 6, 2017 (thank you, President Trump, Ambassador David Melech Friedman and Jared Kushner and Ivanka Trump), THE EVENTS THAT BEGIN THE 70TH WEEK COULD HAPPEN ANY TIME. In this final period Satan will undertake a last great effort to preserve his kingdom over all the earth. Prophet Daniel describes the antichrist's dominion in Daniel 7:7 as "dreadful, terrifying and extremely strong." World-wide troubles and disturbances will begin mildly and increase in intensity as the last week, which is 7 years, progresses. Jesus told His disciples that "there will be a great tribulation, such as has not occurred since the beginning of the world until now, nor ever shall. And unless those days had been cut short (NOT EXEMPT!), no life would have been saved, but for the sake of the elect (Jewish and Gentile believers in Christ) those days shall be cut short" Matthew 24:22.

The prophecy continues with Christ's birth of a Jewish virgin, called Maryam (Mary in Greek), "Therefore the Lord Himself will give you (Jewish people) a sign: Behold, a virgin will be with child and bear a son, and she will call His name Immanuel" (Hebrew for God With Us), Isaiah 7:14.

More prophecies regarding Messiah Jesus:

- Christ being a descendant of Abraham, Isaac, and Jacob, " Genesis 12:3, Genesis 17:19, Numbers 24:17;

- Christ being from the tribe of Judah, "The scepter shall not depart from Judah, nor the ruler's staff from between his feet, until SHILOH (Messianic title) comes , AND TO HIM SHALL BE THE OBEDIENCE OF THE PEOPLES" Genesis 49:10. Jesus is described as "the Lion that is from the tribe of Judah, the Root of David" in Revelation 5:5. Judah was the son of the Patriarch Jacob and his wife Leah. He is the ancestor of Christ in Matthew 1:3-16.

- Christ being anointed and eternal, "Thy throne, O God, is forever and ever; A scepter of uprightness is the scepter of Thy kingdom. Thou hast loved righteousness, and hated wickedness; THEREFORE GOD, THY GOD, HAS ANOINTED THEE WITH THE OIL OF JOY ABOVE THY FELLOWS. Psalm 45:6,7 also Psalm 102:25-27.

- Christ betrayed for 30 pieces of silver, Zechariah 11:12,13, "And I said to them, "If it is good in your sight, give me my wages; but if not, never mind!" So they weighed out THIRTY SHEKELS OF SILVER AS MY WAGES. Then the Lord said to me , "Throw it to the potter, that MAGNIFICENT PRICE AT WHICH I WAS VALUED BY THEM." SO I TOOK THE THIRTY SHEKELS OF SILVER

AND THREW THEM TO THE POTTER IN THE HOUSE OF THE LORD."

- Christ rejected, despised,and forsaken by His own people, Isaiah, Chapter 53. Earlier, in Chapter 52:13-15, God is speaking about Jesus Christ Whom He describes as the Exalted Servant; "Behold, My servant will prosper, He will be high and lifted up, and greatly exalted." Isaiah goes on to describe Christ's sadistic beatings before crucifixion: "Just as many were astonished at you, My people, so His (Jesus') appearance was marred more than any men, and His form more than the sons of men." The night before Jesus was condemned to death by crucifixion, He was arrested and endured 6 trials - 3 Jewish and 3 Roman: "So the Roman cohort and the commander, and the officers of the Jews, arrested Jesus and bound Him, and led Him to Annas first; for he was father-in-law of Caiaphas, who was high priest that year" John 18:12. So the trial before Annas in John 18:12-14, 19-23 was the first Jewish trial of Jesus Christ. The next trial was before Caiaphas (all four Gospels record this trial: Matthew 26:57-68; Mark 14:53-65; Luke 22:54, 63-65; John 18:24. The trial before the Sanhedrin took place "as soon as it was day" Luke 22:66. Jesus again referred to Himself as the Son of Man sitting at the right hand of power, a clear reference to Himself as Messiah. After that Jesus was delivered to the Roman leader Pilate for trial. Pilate found nothing worthy of death to condemn, sending Jesus to King Herod. The trial before Herod is recorded in Luke 23:6-12. Herod hoped to see a miracle, though Jesus answered none of the charges against Him. Herod and his guard mocked Jesus and sent Him back to Pilate with a kingly robe. The second trial before Pilate resulted in Pilate's claim that he had nothing to do with the punishment of Jesus, leaving the fate of Jesus to the crowd in the form of allowing them to choose freedom for Jesus or to release a known criminal named Barabbas. All of that happening at Passover when the crowd chose Barabbas and rejected Jesus shouting: "Crucify! Crucify!" Thus Jesus was condemned to Roman crucifixion. It should be mentioned that five main Jewish laws were unceremoniously broken in the process of the trial: 1) No trial was to be held during the Passover week, 2) Each member of the Sanhedrin (Lower Sanhedrin consisted of 23 judges and Upper Sanhedrin consisted of 71 judges) was to vote INDIVIDUALLY. In Jesus's trial 94 judges voted as a group. 3) the Jews had no authority to execute a person, yet Pilate consented based on their verdict. 4) Trials were not to be held at night, yet Jesus was arrested and tried at night, 5) And according to the Hebrew Law the accused was to be given a defense representative (attorney), though Jesus had no one to represent Him. Ultimately, the trials and death of Jesus Christ were ILLEGAL according to earthly laws and a mockery of the perfect, sinless Messiah. Isaiah concludes that Jesus Christ " will sprinkle many nations, kings will shut their mouths on account of Him; for what had not been told them they will see, and what they had not heard they will understand." Isaiah 52:15.

- Christ mocked and pierced, Psalm 22:7,8,16-18, "All who see me sneer at me; They separate with the lip, they wag the head, saying, "Commit yourself to the Lord; let Him deliver him; let Him rescue him, because He delights in him." "For

203

dogs have surrounded me; a band of evildoers has encompassed me, THEY PIERCED MY HANDS AND MY FEET. I can count all my bones. They look, they stare at me; They divide my garments among them, And for my clothing they cast lots."

All these along with over 300 other Old Testament prophecies were fulfilled in Jesus Christ. Mathematics and Astronomy Professor Peter W. Stoner has made the statement that the chances of just eight prophecies (like these) coming true by sheer chance is 1 in 10 to the seventeenth power (100,000,000,000,000,000). That would be equivalent to covering the whole state of Texas with silver dollars two feet deep and then expecting a blindfolded man to walk across the state and on the very first try find the ONE coin you marked.

Theologians argue that approximately 100 years ago there was hardly a single definite sign regarding the Second Coming of our Lord. Today, however, the Signs of Christ's soon coming and the End of the Age are strikingly evident. Signs of the End Times are all over us. They are so many and in such an abundance and intensity that they are like pulsating neon lights in heaven proclaiming that Jesus Christ is soon COMING BACK.

Let me be specific: The first sign that indicated Christ's soon glorious, visible return happend on November 2, 1917 when the British government issued the BALFOUR Declaration in the form of a letter from the United Kingdom's Foreign Secretary, Arthur James Balfour, to Lionel Walter Rothschild, who was President of the British Zionist Organization. The letter expressed the British support for "the establishment in Palestine of a national home for the Jewish people." The Balfour Declaration electrified evangelical Christians of England, because they knew that according to the series of prophecies of the Old Testament, God will gather His people from all the nations and bring them into their Promised Land BEFORE Christ's Return.

Here are some of the prophesies regarding the Restoration of Israel that were later fulfilled when Israel became a State on May 14, 1948 (Israel became a nation in 1312 B.C.--more than two thousand years before the rise of Islam).

Prophet Ezekiel (his name in Hebrew means God Strengthens) writes in 590 B.C. "For thus says the Lord God, Behold, I Myself will search for My sheep and seek them out. As the shepherd cares for his herd in the day when he is among his scattered sheep, so I will care for My sheep and will deliver them from all the places to which they were scattered on a cloudy and gloomy day. And I will bring them out from the peoples and gather them from the countries and bring them to their OWN LAND; and I will feed them on the mountains of ISRAEL, by the streams, and in all the inhabited places of the land" Ezekiel 34:11-13.

Writes Prophet Isaiah (his name in Hebrew means Jehovah is salvation) 700 B.C. "Then it will happen on that day that the Lord will again recover the SECOND TIME with His hand the remnant of His people, who will remain, From Assyria, Egypt, Pathros (Southland/Upper Egypt), Cush (Ethiopia), Elam (an ancient nation connected with Media), Shinar (the region around Iraq), Hamath (Israelites exiled to Samaria), And from the islands of the sea (for Prophet Isaiah who knew of only three continents, but prophesied in 700 B.C. about the "islands of the sea" which today are represented by Australia, New Zealand, Canada and North and South America). And He will lift up a standard for the nations, and will assemble the banished ones of Israel and will gather the dispersed of Judah, from the four corners of the earth" Isaiah 11:11,12.

Writes Prophet Jeremiah (his name in Hebrew means Jehovah establishes) 650 B.C. "For I know the plans that I have for you, declares the Lord, plans for welfare and not for calamity to give you a future and a hope. Then you will call upon Me and come and pray to Me, and I will listen to you. And you will seek Me and find Me, when you search for Me with all your heart. And I will restore your fortunes, and will gather you from all the nations and from all the places where I have driven you, declares the Lord, and I will bring you back to the place from where I sent you into exile"

Jeremiah 29:11-14.

The second historic Sign took place on December 11th, 1917 when British General Edmund Allenby, who was a deeply religious man, entered Jerusalem thus liberating the Holy City from a 400 year Turkish rule. That day, General Allenby got off his white horse and entered Jerusalem on foot. He knew that according to Revelation 19:11 the Messiah Jesus at His Second Coming will come out of heaven on a white horse, "And I (John) saw heaven opened; and behold a white horse, and He who sat upon it is called Faithful and True; and in righteousness He judges and wages war."

One hundred three years have passed since that time. Israel became a nation in 1948, and 19 years later, in the Six-Day War of 1967, between Israel and the Arab states of Egypt, Syria and Jordan, Israel seized the Sinai Peninsula and the Gaza Strip from Egypt, the West Bank and East Jerusalem from Jordan, and the Golan Heights from Syria. By recapturing Jerusalem (which in Hebrew means Possession of Peace) Israelites fulfilled the century's old prophecy.

December 6, 2017 President Trump recognized Jerusalem as "an eternal capital of the Jewish people" and ordered the planning of the relocation of the U.S. Embassy in Israel from Tel Aviv to Jerusalem. It should be noted that President Trump's decision was rejected by a majority of world leaders. The United Nations Security Council held an emergency meeting on December 7th, where 14 out of 15 members condemned Trump's decision, but the motion was vetoed by the U.S. Britain, France, Sweden, Italy, and Japan were among the countries that criticized Trump's decision at the "emergency meeting" (not to mention American liberal politicians and the press corps that openly ridiculed our President and accused him of "aggravating the already fragile Middle East situation").

The location of the relocated Embassy was decided to be at the former site of its Consular General in the Arnona neighborhood, in West Jerusalem. I remember visiting that area in December, 1984 with a group of evangelical pastors from New York and Minnesota. There were a number of former Soviet Jews living in Arnona.

On May 14th, 2018 the United States officially opened its Embassy in Jerusalem, Israel, 70 years to the day that President Truman recognized Israel as an independent country, making the United States the first nation to do so. (The estimated five year construction period with an estimated 7-10 million dollar price ticket was actually achieved in a little over five months for a total cost of only $400,000 under the direct guidance of our President). Our President knows a thing or two about construction and real estate, you know.

Two hundred fifty rabbis sent President Trump a letter saying, "You will be eternally remembered in the history of the Jewish people." The Head Rabbi of Israel, Itsak Josef, commented, "You, Mister President, have the rare privilege to be the first American President recognizing Jerusalem to be the eternal capital of the Jewish State." When I ask my Jewish American friends, "Do you know that the United States of America is in the middle of Jerusalem?" The usual answer is: "Oy vey! Whaaat?" Then I suggest for them to spell "JerUSAlem").

You see, in Genesis 12 the Lord said to Abram (whom He renamed Abraham which means Father of the multitude of nations in Genesis 17:5):
"And I will make you a great nation,
And I will bless you,
And make your name great,
And so you shall be a blessing;
I will BLESS those who BLESS you,
And the one who CURSES you I will curse,
And in you ALL THE FAMILIES OF THE EARTH SHALL BE BLESSED." verses 2,3.

Presently, under President Trump's Administration, the United States is exhibiting unwavering strong support for the only true democracy in the Middle East, namely, the State of Israel. And according to God's words in Genesis "I will bless those who bless you," the U.S. is currently blessed with the President who has been called "America's First Zionist President" after his new Peace Plan Proposal for the Middle East.

The historic and groundbreaking peace treaties between the United Arab Emirates, Bahrain and Israel were signed September 16, 2020 marking the "dawn of a new Middle East" said Prime Minister Benjamin Netanyahu. "Jews have prayed for peace for thousands of years and the citizens of Israel have for decades. This day brings hope to all of the children of Abraham."

President Trump called it "an incredible day for the world." "The courage of the Israeli and Arab leaders has enabled these countries to take a major stride toward a future where people of all faiths live together in peace and prosperity" he added. Supposedly up to five other Arab nations are planning to follow the Peace Plan and sign their treaties with Israel after the U.S. elections. On September 9th, 2020 President Donald J.Trump was nominated for the 2021 Nobel Peace Prize for his leadership in brokering the Abraham Accords. (Since then our President was nominated two more times, the latest by Australian law professors for a total of three nominations. "What he has done with the Trump Doctrine is that he has decided he would no longer have America in endless wars, wars which achieve nothing but the killing of thousands of young Americans." Professor David Flint, September 28, 2020).

The recent unprecedented economic growth in the U.S. is, to a large extent, the result of America's RENEWED support of Israel. God blesses those who bless "His people Israel." Today's Coronavirus disrupted and considerably slowed down the U.S. economy and is threatening the rest of the world. Now, as never before, America needs to pray for God's mercy to "heal the land" spiritually, and also from this pandemic outbreak. "If my people who are called by My name humble themselves and pray, and seek my face and turn from their wicked ways, THEN I will hear from heaven, will forgive their sin, and will heal their land" 2 Chronicles 7:14.

It should be noted that the worst American relations with Israel, since the birth of that nation on May 14th, 1948, was attributed to the eight year reign of the 44th President, Barack Hussein Obama (2008-2016). The open animosity toward the Prime Minister of Israel, Benjamin Netanyahu and the refusal to attend Netanyahu's speech to Congress by both President Obama and Vice-President Biden, March 1, 2015, where Netanyahu warned the Administration about the danger of the Iran Nuclear Deal, will go down in the annals of American diplomatic history as a gross underestimation of Iran's quest to obtain nuclear weapons. Iran has resumed uranium enrichment at its underground Fordow facility, taking the next step in its stage-by-stage move away from its nuclear deal with the West as of November 2019.

At the time of this writing, Iran is fast becoming a business and military partner with Communist China and Russia. In fact they are buying weapons from them. Both Iran and China are U.S. adversaries, not to mention Russia. Prophet Ezekiel, his Hebrew name means Jehovah strengthens, prophesied in the early years of the Babylonian exile, between 592-570 B.C. that at the end of the age Persia, called Iran in 1935, will attack Israel along with five other countries: Gog Magog-prince of Rosh, Meshech, and Tubal identified as Russia; (the etymological root of the name Russia is of Hebrew origin--Rosh); Cush, or Ethiopia; Put, or Libya; Gomer; and Beth-togarmah, believed to be lands of Allemagne and northern parts of Turkey. These countries are listed as Israel's adversaries. "After many days...in the latter years you (the above mentioned countries) will come into the land that is restored from the sword, whose inhabitants have been gathered from many nations to the mountains of Israel which had been a continual waste; but its people were brought out from the nations, and they are living securely, all of them." Ezekiel 38:8.

This fascinating prophecy covers chapters 38 and 39, and describes in detail how invaders will be destroyed by the Almighty God of Israel: "You shall fall on the mountains of Israel, you and all your troops, and the peoples who are with you (talking about Gog Magog that will be the leading army). "You will fall on the open field; for it is I who have spoken, declares the Lord God. And I shall send fire upon Magog and those who inhabit the coastlands in safety" Ezekiel 39:6. It should be mentioned that Ezekiel wrote this prophecy in 537 B.C. and knew of only three continents. "Coastlands" for him are present day Canada, North and South America, Australia etc.). It is a sobering thought that God "shall send fire... on "those who inhabit the coastlands in safety" - another translation from King James Bible "those who dwell carelessly in the isles." "Behold, it is coming and it shall be done," declares the Lord God. "That is the day of which I have spoken" verse 8. "Those who inhabit the cities of Israel will go out and make fires with the weapons (of all destroyed invading armies) and burn them...and for SEVEN YEARS they will make fires of them." verse 9. "And it will come about on that day that I shall give Gog a burial ground there in Israel, the valley of those who pass by east of the sea, and it will block the passers-by. So they will bury Gog there with all his multitude, and they will call it the valley of Hamon-gog (which literally means "Valley of the multitudes of Gog).

I will explain why I am writing what I am writing and how it is connected with the above verse. When in 1984 our group visited Israel on the way to Jordan, Egypt, and Greece we visited the famous ancient first century stone fortress in the Southern District of Israel called Masada. It is located high above the Dead Sea on a tall rocky mesa. Masada was the site of the Jewish people's last stand against the Romans after the fall of Jerusalem in 70 A.D.

As a side note, after visiting Masada our bus tour took us to the Dead Sea beach. Water in the Dead Sea is 10 times as salty as the ocean. They say you can't drown in the Dead Sea even if you tried - it is so heavy with salt that one becomes very buoyant and it's difficult to even put your foot on the bottom. Think again! The Dead Sea was named the SECOND most dangerous place to swim in Israel. People, mostly unsuspecting tourists, actually drown in the Dead Sea. The salt and rich mineral content of the water contribute to drowning deaths because even a few swallows of it destroys the electrolyte balance in the body. In other words, people poison themselves with salt. I did not know about it in

December of 1984. When we arrived at the Dead Sea beach I plunged in the water and swam for about 15 - 20 feet on one breath, my face under the water. When I came out to catch air my eyes were burning from the salt and it seemed like there was no air left to breathe. I got scared. I remember turning on my back and swimming back to the shore as fast as I could. The beach had several showers and I ran to the closest one moaning in pain. I was told my eyes were bright red.

Please bear with me. After my horrific swimming experience our group was planning to go and see the historic valley of Hamon-gog. It was located "east of the sea," "sea" being the Dead Sea. It took us half an hour or so to get to that valley. It did not have a single Jewish kibbutz (a collective community in Israel that was traditionally based on agriculture). Our guide Yakov, Israeli Air Force fighter pilot reservist, told us that this valley is "cursed." When we asked him why? (being aware of the text in Ezekiel, Chapters 38,39), Yakov, who said he was "not religious," replied that his grandpa, who was a Rabbi, told him long ago that the Valley of Hamon-gog is the place where Israelis will be "burying the Russian hordes." We showed Yakov the place in the Old Testament, in the Book of Ezekiel 39:11 and 15 that describes the destruction of invading armies led by Gog-Magog. He was awe stricken that the future events were predicted by the Lord through Prophet Ezekiel just as his grandpa had told him. For Yakov and all other Jewish people, whom I know personally and who tell me that they are "not religious," there is verse 22 of the same Chapter 39: "And the house of Israel will know that I am the Lord their God from THAT DAY ONWARD." That is after the Lord God will utterly destroy all invading armies led by Gog of the land of Magog - Russia, which will attack Israel "after many days, in the latter years." Prophet Ezekiel concludes Chapter 39 with a magnificent promise for the Jewish people: "And I will not hide My face from them any longer, for I shall have poured out My Spirit on the house of Israel," declares the Lord God."

The Critical Importance Of Jerusalem

It is important to understand that almost all events of world history revolve in some way around the people and land of Israel. Its historic capital, Jerusalem, was originally called Salem - Peace in the Bible as early as Genesis 14:18. Its name was later changed to Jerusalem when David became king and ruled there for 33 years over all Israel and Judah, 2 Samuel 5:5,6. In verse 9 David called Jerusalem "the city of David." By all historic accounts Jerusalem is the world's oldest city with over 3,000 year old history. Here are some names in the Old Testament applying to Jerusalem: City of God, Zion, City of Judah, City of David, Holy City, Faithful City, City of Righteousness, City of Truth, City of the Great King. Jerusalem is mentioned 806 times--660 times in the Old Testament and 146 times in the New Testament.

The Old Testament Prophet Zechariah (his name in Hebrew means The Lord Remembers) prophesied 520 B.C.,

"Sing for joy and be glad, O daughter of Zion; for behold I am coming and I will dwell in your midst," declares the Lord. And many nations will join themselves to the Lord in that day and will become my people. Then I will dwell in your midst, and you will know that the Lord of hosts has sent Me to you. And the Lord will possess Judah as His portion in the holy land, AND WILL AGAIN CHOOSE JERUSALEM. Thus says the Lord, I will return to Zion and will dwell in the midst of Jerusalem. Then Jerusalem will be called the City of Truth, and the mountain of the Lord of hosts will be called the Holy Mountain. Thus says the Lord of hosts, Behold, I am going to save My people from the land of the EAST and from the land of the WEST; and I will bring them back, and they will live in the midst of Jesusalem, and they will be My people and I will be their God in truth and righteousness. And it will come about that just as you were a curse among the nations, O house of Judah and house of Israel, so I will save you that you may become a blessing. Do not fear; let your hands be strong. For thus says the Lord of hosts, Just as I purposed to do harm to you when your fathers provoked Me to wrath, says the Lord of hosts, and I have not relented, so I have again purposed in these days to do good to Jerusalem and to the house of Judah. Do not fear!" Zechariah 2:10-12, 8:3,7,8,13-15.

Prophet Micah (in Hebrew his name means Who is like the Lord prophesied 750 B.C. regarding Peaceful Latter Days:
"And many nations will come and say,
Come and let us go up to the mountains of the Lord
And to the house of the God of Jacob,
And that He may teach us about His ways
And that we may walk in His paths."
For from Zion will go forth the Law,
Even the word of the Lord from Jerusalem"
Micah 4:2.

Prophet Isaiah (whose name in Hebrew means Jehovah Is Salvation) prophesied 730 B.C. regarding Jerusalem's glory and New Name in Chapter 62. Here are several verses from this remarkable Chapter:
"For Zion's sake I will not keep silent,
And for Jerusalem's sake I will not keep quiet,
Until her righteousness goes forth like brightness,
And her salvation like a torch that is burning,
And the nations will see your righteousness,
And all kings your glory;
And you will be called by a new name,
Which the mouth of the Lord will designate.

And you will be a crown of beauty in the hand of the Lord,
And a royal diadem in the hand of your God.
On your walls, O Jerusalem, I have appointed watchmen;
All day and all night they will never keep silent.
You who remind the Lord, take no rest for yourselves;
And give Him no rest until He establishes
And makes JERUSALEM A PRAISE IN THE EARTH.
Behold, the Lord has proclaimed to the end of the earth,
Say to the daughter of Zion, "Lo, your salvation comes;
Behold His reward is with Him."
And they will call them , "The holy people,
The redeemed of the Lord";
And you will be called, "Sought out, a CITY NOT
FORSAKEN"
Isaiah 62:1-3,6,7,11,12.

Trump's Election

I vividly remember Monday, September 26, 2016, when the then Presidential contender Donald J.Trump promised that if elected, "We will move the American Embassy (from Tel-Aviv) to the eternal capital of the Jewish people, Jerusalem." Our President made good on his promise: "Today we officially opened the United States Embassy in Jerusalem. For many years we failed to acknowledge the obvious, the plain reality that Israel's capital is Jerusalem," Donald Trump, May 14, 2018. IT IS PROPHETIC! I honestly stand on record that on that memorable September 26 afternoon I was telling my family and friends that Mr. Trump is our next President according to the above prophetic Scriptures. Lord knows I was doubted not only by the majority of my friends but also by my own family, who said "please don't say that Trump is going to win. People will laugh at you, thinking you are crazy!"

When "shoe-in" Hillary Clinton was already planning her big victory celebration with fireworks over

215

the Hudson River on November 7, 2016, the God of Abraham, Isaac and Jacob Who revealed Himself in His Son, Jesus Christ, and Whose "thoughts are not your thoughts, neither are your ways My ways" Isaiah 55:8, obviously HAD OTHER PLANS.

End Times

In view of current events in the world, and the growing lawlessness and turmoil in America in particular, Christians are seeking for answers from the Word of God. The Old Testament Prophet Amos said: "Surely the Lord God does nothing unless He reveals His secret counsel to His servants the prophets" Amos 3:7. I would like to suggest a method that helped me to better understand the text of the Scriptures since I have been a student of prophecy for over 40 years. "Face Value Hermeneutics" is a theological concept which argues that Scripture is best interpreted by Scripture. In other words, the Bible in its entirety explains itself. The word Eschatology - "eschatos" (Greek) meaning "last" and "logy" meaning "the study of" is a part of theology that deals with Final Events of history and the ultimate destiny of humanity. This concept is commonly referred to as the End Times.

When Jesus was sitting on the Mount of Olives, His disciples came to Him privately and asked Him, "Tell us, when will these things be, and what will be the sign of Your coming, and of the end of the age" Matthew 24:3. The disciples knew Jesus was COMING BACK. He told them not to be misled by anyone, because "many will come in My name, saying, 'I am the Christ,' and will mislead many." Then Jesus told them that they "will be hearing of wars and rumors of wars; see that you are not frightened, for those things must take place, but that is not yet the end. For nation will rise against nation, and kingdom against kingdom, and in various places there will be famines, and earthquakes" verses 6,7.

This prophecy dealt with future events because at that time the Roman Empire was ruling the world and was invincible till 476 A.D. Consequently the verse in Matthew 24:7 "For nation will rise against nation, and kingdom against kingdom" could not have been fulfilled during the disciples' lifetime. The events described in the above verse remind us of the current world situation with its more than 60 local wars and conflicts.

Then in verse 9 we read that "Then they will deliver You to tribulation ("Thlipsis Megales"- Great Tribulation in Greek. "Thlipsis" means "attrition,squeezing"), and kill You, and You will be hated by all nations on account of My name." Jesus uses YOU three times. Who is Jesus talking about? Is it Israel or the Church of God? The answer is in the last words of the verse "on account of My name." Who to this very day are called by His name? (the name "Christians" originated in Antioch, Syria , "...and the disciples were first called Christians in Antioch" Acts 11:26b). God's children, born again Christian believers, for whom "the knowledge of Christ and the power of His resurrection and the fellowship of His sufferings, being conformed to His death, in order that I (we) may attain to the resurrection from the dead," is the very essence and goal of their/mine earthly life. It was so for Apostle Paul in Phillippians 3:10,11.

It is those in Christ Jesus, for whom "neither circumcision nor uncircumcision means anything, but faith working through love" Galatians 5:6. It is those who are in Christ and are called by Paul "a new creation"---"poema" in Greek, because "the old things passed away; behold, new things have come" 2 Corinthians 5:17.

In verse 12 Jesus describes today's world state of affairs, and might I add, the current situation in our

217

country: "And because lawlessness is increased, most people's love will grow cold." Verse 13 encourages believers to be faithful to the end: "But the one who endures to the end, he shall be saved." This verse echoes the words of Jesus Christ in Revelation 2:10b: "Be faithful until death, and I will give you the crown of life."

Verse 14 proclaims that "This gospel of the kingdom shall be preached in the whole world for the witness to all the nations, and THEN the end shall come." First the entire world will have to hear the GOOD NEWS of salvation through Jesus Christ, and Him alone, "THEN (not BEFORE) the end shall come."

The Biblical sequence of apocalyptic events include: the coming of the beast "from the Sea" who is the antichrist and "the beast from the Earth"-- a false prophet, Revelation, Chapter 13. The rule of antichrist for 42 months is known as the Great Tribulation period, (second part of seven year period) and the wrath of Satan: "And there was given to him (antichrist) a mouth speaking arrogant words and blasphemies; and authority to act for 42 months (3.5 years) was given to him," " And it was given to him (antichrist) to make war with the saints (believers in Christ) and to overcome them; and authority over every tribe and people and tongue and nation was given to him" Revelation 13:5,7. "Woe to the earth and the sea, because the devil (satan) has come down to you, having GREAT WRATH, knowing that he has only short time" Revelation 12:12.

Then we have the glorious return of our Savior Jesus Christ: "BUT IMMEDIATELY AFTER - "akrivos meta" in Greek (NOT BEFORE) the tribulation of those days the son will be darkened, and the moon will not give its light, and the stars will fall from the sky, and the powers of the heavens will be shaken and THEN the sign of the son of man (Jesus) will appear in the sky, and

THEN all the tribes of the earth will mourn, and they will see the Son of Man coming on the clouds of the sky with power and great glory. And He will send forth his angels with a great trumpet and they will gather together ("episunagoge" in Greek) His elect (Jewish and Gentile believers in Christ) from the four winds, from one end of the sky to the other" Matthew 24:29-31. This is a graphic description of the Rapture of the church according to Jesus Christ.

Back to the two beasts of Revelation 13. The false prophet (second beast) will "exercise all the authority of the first beast in his presence and he makes the earth and those who dwell in it to worship the first beast (antichrist), whose fatal wound was healed." The false prophet will "perform great signs, so that he even makes fire come down out of heaven to the earth in the presence of men" Verses 12,13. The false prophet will tell " those who dwell on the earth to make an image to the beast who had the wound of the sword and has come to life." The false prophet will "give breath to the image of the beast, that the image of the beast might even speak and cause as many as do not worship the image of the beast to be killed" Verses 14,15.

There will be believers during the 42 months reign of antichrist (Revelation 13:5) who will not worship the beast and who will be killed. These are martyrs whose souls we see on the altar after the Lamb (Jesus) broke the fifth seal: "And when He broke the fifth seal, I (John) saw underneath the altar the souls of those who had been slain BECAUSE OF THE WORD OF GOD, AND BECAUSE OF THE TESTIMONY WHICH THEY HAD MAINTAINED" Revelation 6:9. We see these heroes of faith along with "their fellow servants and their brethren who were to be killed even as they had been" Revelation 6:11 in the next chapter. "After these things I looked, and behold a great multitude, which no one could count, from every nation and all tribes and peoples and tongues, standing before the throne and before the Lamb (Jesus Christ), clothed in white robes, and palm branches were in their hands."

They were glorifying God and the Lamb of God, Jesus crying out with a loud voice: "Salvation to our God who sits on the throne, and to the Lamb." One of the elders asked John,

"These who are, clothed in white robes, who are they, and from where have they come?" John did not know answering, "My lord, you know." The elder said to him and to US WHO READ THESE WORDS: "These are the ones who come out of the great tribulation, and they have washed their robes and made them white in the blood of the Lamb." Revelation 7:9,10,13,14.

Now, remember the people who did not worship the image of the beast and therefore were killed? Revelation 13:15? We meet them again in Revelation 20:4, "And I saw thrones, and they sat upon them, and judgement was given to them. And I saw the souls of those who had been beheaded because of the testimony of Jesus and because of the word of God, and those who had not worshiped the beast or his image, and had not received the mark upon their forehead and upon their hand (666); and they came to life and reigned with Christ for a thousand years."

Do you doubt yet that what we are reading describes the courageous Christians from every corner of the world?   Didn't Jesus say that "the gospel of the kingdom shall be preached IN THE WHOLE WORLD FOR THE WITNESS TO ALL THE NATIONS?" Matthew 24:14. WARNING! When I led a series on The End Times at the New Life Baptist Church in Hollywood, Florida I had a chance to talk to a number of young couples with small kids. I was asked about Revelation, chapter 13,. regarding verses 16 and 17: "And he (false prophet) causes all, the small and the great, and the rich and the poor, and the free men and the slaves, to be given a mark on their right hand, or on their forehead. And he provides that NO ONE SHOULD BE ABLE TO BUY OR SELL, EXCEPT THE ONE WHO HAS THE MARK, EITHER THE NAME OF THE BEAST (antichrist) OR THE NUMBER OF HIS NAME." So the question was: "if we do not receive the mark of the beast, provided the church will go through the period of testing and will not be raptured before the tribulation, we will not be able to feed our family and we will eventually die. What if we receive the mark but in our hearts believe in God? That way we will spare our children from dying of hunger." I then asked that young mom how long she was planning to exist feeding her family, remembering that antichrist will be given authority to act for 42 months (which is 3.5 years). She had to agree: "42 months" she said. Then reasoning from Scripture we came to a conclusion that afterwards (after 42 months of antichrist's rule) comes the wrath of God on all those who "worship the beast and his image, and RECEIVE A MARK on his (her) forehead or upon his hand, he also will drink of the wine of the wrath of God, which is mixed in full strength in the cup of His anger; and he will be tormented with fire and brimstone in the presence of holy angels and in the presence of the Lamb (Jesus). And the smoke of their torment goes up forever and ever and they have no rest day and night, those who worship the beast and his image, and WHOEVER RECEIVES THE MARK OF HIS NAME. Here is the PERSEVERANCE OF THE SAINTS who keep the commandments of God and their faith in Jesus. And I (John) heard the voice from heaven, saying, "Write, 'Blessed are the dead who die in the Lord FROM NOW ON!'" "Yes , says the Spirit, "that they may rest from their labors, for their deeds follow with them'" Revelation 14:9-13. It was an emotional moment.

Couples realised that compromise will have eternal consequences. We prayed and agreed that "to such (children) belongs the kingdom of God" Mark 10:14, and that we are to "Be faithful until death, and I (Jesus) will give you the crown of life" Revelation 2:10b. Humanly speaking, I can see how young mothers will be pleading with their husbands at the end of the age "for the sake of our children" to receive the mark of the beast and live (again only for 3.5 years) according to Revelation 13:5. I totally see it in the families where one of the spouses is not a Christian. They obviously do not know better and will, Lord forbid, try to push their Christian husbands/wives to receive the mark "for the sake of the family and children." For those who do not believe and acknowledge Jesus Christ as their personal Lord and Savior there is still time to repent of their sin of unbelief and ask Jesus in your heart. Your decision will determine where you will spend eternity. Remember, "that if you confess with your mouth Jesus as Lord, and believe in your heart that God raised Him from the dead, you shall be saved; for with the heart man (woman) believes, resulting in righteousness, and with the mouth he (she) confesses, resulting in salvation." "Whoever will call upon the name of the Lord will be saved" Romans 10:9,10,13. Make your decision TODAY! For "Tomorrow is not promised to anyone."

In His parable about tares and wheat in Matthew 13, (tares, the sons of the evil one-- satan), and wheat, sons of the kingdom-- born again Christians), Jesus explains that BOTH WILL GROW TOGETHER UNTIL THE HARVEST. "Allow both to grow together until the HARVEST (the Rapture of the church of Christ); and in the time of the harvest I (Jesus) will say to the reapers: (in Revelation 14, they are Angels accompanied by the Son of Man--Jesus, verses 14-19), "First gather up the tares and bind them in bundles to burn them up; but gather the wheat into my barn" Matthew 13:30. If believers in Christ are raptured and the nonbelievers have 7 more years on earth, HOW is that both "growing" (living) together until the harvest, the end of the world?

Believers will not be raptured before the Great Tribulation BUT AFTER, just like what Jesus said in Matthew 24:29, "IMMEDIATELY AFTER THE TRIBULATION of those days" BEFORE "THE WRATH OF GOD" Apostle Paul wrote in I Thessalonians about the Church and its future: "For the Lord Himself will descend from heaven (His second coming) with a shout, with the voice of the archangel, and with the trumpet of God; and the dead in Christ shall rise first. Then we who are ALIVE and REMAIN (till Christ's coming and the Rapture of the Church), shall be caught up together with them (those who died in Jesus) in the clouds to meet the Lord in the air, and thus we shall always be with the Lord" Chapter 4:16,17. ALIVE and REMAIN suggests that Christians will not be raptured BEFORE the Great Tribulation. Christ appears after the Tribulation at which time the Rapture of the Church will take place with those who have REMAINED and survived the Great Tribulation.

When Apostle Paul wrote to Corinthians, he said, "Behold, I tell you a mystery; WE SHALL NOT ALL SLEEP (die), but we shall be changed, in a moment, in the twinkling of an eye, at the last trumpet (we find this last trumpet in Revelation 11:15; "And the seventh angel sounded; and there arose loud voices in heaven, saying, "The kingdom of the world has become the kingdom of our Lord, and of his Christ; and He will reign forever and ever"), FOR THE TRUMPET WILL SOUND, AND THE DEAD WILL BE RAISED IMPERISHABLE, AND WE SHALL BE CHANGED"
1 Corinthians 15:51,52.

In 2 Thessalonians, Chapter 2, Apostle Paul teaches the church that before the coming of Christ and the Rapture of the Church, apostasy comes first, and the man of lawlessness (antichrist) will be revealed, "Now we request you, brethren, with regard to the coming of our Lord Jesus Christ (His second visible coming, parousia - Greek), and our gathering together to Him (Rapture of the church, episunagoge, harpazo in Greek), that you may not be quickly shaken from your composure or be disturbed either by the spirit or a message or a letter as if from us, to the effect that the day of the Lord has come. LET NO ONE IN ANY WAY DECEIVE YOU FOR IT WILL NOT COME UNLESS THE APOSTASY COMES FIRST , and the man of lawlessness is revealed, the son of destruction (antichrist)" 2 Thessalonians 2:1-4.

Dear Brothers and Sisters in our soon coming Jesus,
may we remember the words of Apostle Paul who wrote to the church in Philippi, "For to me, to live is Christ, and to die is gain...For to you it has been granted for Christ's sake, not only to believe in Him, But also to suffer for His sake" Philippians 1:21,29.

FINAL REFLECTIONS

As I look back on my life I realize how much the Lord Jesus blessed me and kept me safe all those years. I count my blessings as the classic Christian hymn goes, "Count your many blessings, name them one by one. Count your blessings, see what God has done." I would like to thank the Lord Jesus Who inspired me to write this book and Who continues to encourage me to look up to Him for answers in my earthly pilgrimage. I am thankful for Your reminder to abide in You, "Abide in Me, and I in you. As the branch cannot bear fruit of itself, unless it abides in the vine, so neither can you, unless you abide in Me.

I am the vine, you are the branches; he who abides in Me, and I in him, he bears much fruit; for apart from Me you can do nothing" John 15:4,5.

My Prayer

Dear Heavenly Father,

It is through Your Son Jesus that I come before Your holy face. I am so thankful that You revealed Yourself to me and brought me into a personal relationship with Your Son Jesus Christ, my Savior, Counselor, and Redeemer of my eternal soul. You gave me a loving wife, a mother of our four beautiful children which is Your gift for both of us, "Behold, children are a gift from the Lord, how blessed is the man whose quiver is full of them," and I thank you for that. I feel blessed in Your presence and in the presence of our children, their spouses and our seven grandchildren. May all of them know, trust and glorify Your holy name, and grow in the grace and knowledge of Your Son's soon glorious and visible return.

I also thank you for my new country-- America, land that I love. Bless, guide and protect her. It still has a lot of Your children who love and magnify Your name. Bless our President and Vice-President and their families. Grant them victory in 2020. May your will be done on earth as it is in heaven.

I pray in the powerful precious name of my personal Lord and Savior Jesus Christ, the soon coming Messiah.

Amen

ADDENDUM

Branitski Ancestors

The ancestors on my father's side go back to Count Franciszek Ksawery Branicki (Polish spelling of Count Francois-Xavier Branitski 1731-1819). Count Branitski was General of Lithuania from 1768–1773, Ambassador to Moscow in 1771, Field Crown Hetman in 1773 and Great Crown Hetman of the Polish-Lithuanian Commonwealth from 1774–1794.

He was gifted vast estates in Bila Tserkva, a city in Central Ukraine, 50 miles south of Kyiv. To this day, one can visit Alexandra Park named after Count Branitski's wife, Countess Alexandra. This park was founded in the late 18th century. It is currently managed by the National Academy of Sciences of Ukraine. I had the opportunity to have a missions outreach in Bila Tserkva in the 1990s at the church where the Branitski family is buried. I am also an Honorary Citizen of the city of Bila Tserkva.

Branitski Coat of Arms

Count Xavier Branitski(1731-1819)

As a side note, our eldest son, Andrei, married Thea who always hoped to have a son for whom she had already chosen a name. When they were blessed with the birth of their first son in 2013 we were surprised to learn that he was named Xavier Branitski. You see, neither Andrei nor Thea knew that our sweet little Xavier had a great, great, great, great, great great grandfather named Count Xavier Branitski.

A bit of trivia regarding our ancestor, the Polish nobleman and general, Count Branitski: In 1766 Count Branitski sustained a serious wound as a result of a pistol duel over an Italian actress in Warsaw with the notorious Casanova, who happened to be in Poland at that time. Both Count Xavier and Cassanova were injured and both survived.

Wife of Count Xavier Branitski
Grand Duchess Countess Alexandra
Branitski (1754-1838)

Alexandra Park, Bila Tserkva, Ukraine

With the Mayor of Bila Tserkva giving me the keys to the city

The following is a bit of history for our children and grandchildren. In 1781 Count Branitski married Aleksandra von Engelhardt (1754-1838), a niece of Prince Potemkin. They had a daughter, Elizabeth (1792-1880), who was married to Field Marshall Prince Mikhail Vorontsov (1782-1856), renowned for his success in the Napoleonic wars. Countess Elizabeth Branitski, a great niece of Potemkin, met Mikhail Vorontsov in Paris when she was 23 and married him there in 1819. Born into one of the oldest Polish families, Countess Elizabeth brought with her a huge family fortune. She and her husband returned to Russia in 1823 where Prince Vorontsov became governor of the Caucasus until 1844. They entertained lavishly at their magnificent palace in Odessa. Princess Branitski Vorontsova was described as one of the most captivating women of her time. She had a sweet, charismatic personality displaying grace and a natural elegance. It is said that many fell head over heels in love with her including the great Russian poet Alexander Pushkin.

Contemporaries wrote that Elizabeth and Prince Vorontsov were the ideal married couple. In actuality, General Vorontsov had several lovers and was a "favorite" of Catherine the Great. Elizabeth was saddened to know about her husband's escapades with other women and is said to have become "close" with the poet Alexander Pushkin who stayed with the Vorontsov family during the summer of 1824. Elizabeth was 32 years old at the time and was enchanted by Pushkin's poetry. Pushkin fell passionately in love with Elizabeth. He was smitten by Elizabeth's kindness, intellectual abilities and beauty. He wrote several poems for her including Talisman, The Burned Letter and The Angel. Princess Elizabeth also served as a prototype of Tatiana Larina in Pushkin's "Evgenii Onegin." Pushkin left Yalta in 1824. Nine months later Elizabeth gave birth to her daughter Sofia (1825-1879).

Princess   Elizabeth   Branitski   Vorontsova (1792-1880)

General, Prince Mikhail Vorontsov, husband of Princess Elizabeth Branitski

Sophia Mikhailovna Shuvalova (1825-1879)
Daughter of Elizabeth Branitski Vorontsova

Alexander Pushkin, rumored to be Sophia's father

Branitski-Vorontsov Palace, Odessa

Branitski-Vorontsov Palace, Alupka, Crimea

The Branitski Chateau Montresor in France was acquired by Polish Count Xavier Branitski (grandson of patriarch Xavier Branitski) in 1849 when he fled Russia to avoid edicts of Tsar Nicholas I.

ADDENDUM

May 1993 "Reflections" Article by Slavic Gospel Association President, Dr. John Aker

Were you to meet this man, after learning something about his life and background, you would most probably want to ask him what could have driven him to abandon a life of prestige and power in the former Soviet

Union. Victor Branitski would certainly answer--the love of a charming and beautiful American woman...Lilli. Theirs is a very special love story...

Victor's parents were typical in one way in that they were Communists. But in other ways, they were not so typical. The father was a colonel in the Soviet army; Victor's mother, a well-educated high school principal in Kiev. They were wise in the ways of the world and well stationed within their own society. Together, they raised Victor in a Communist home devoid of the influence of God's love. As a young man, Victor was an active member of the Komsomol, the Communist Youth League. To him, the story of Jesus was nothing more than a fable--a fairy tale...without reason or relevance. Surely it was to be avoided. As he grew, Victor's considerable talents became quite evident to his parents. He learned music quickly, and at an early age was an accomplished pianist. His language skills blossomed through hard work and privileged education. He was fluent and facile with the English language. He became a first lieutenant in the Soviet army. And, after completing his compulsory military service, became a world-class player on the famed Dynamo soccer team in Kiev, capital city of Ukraine. And that is when he met Lilli--and she soon became all that mattered in his life.

Lilli and Victor were married in Ukraine and Victor immigrated to America with his new bride. After four years in the States, he gave his life to Christ and dedicated himself totally to the Lord's service. While pursuing a successful business career, Victor also gave freely of his energies and resources to the church. He was a leader in both spheres. But, something was missing...

Deep within his own heart, Victor felt the call of his own people. He became involved as a board member at Slavic Gospel Association...served actively with the

John Guest Evangelistic Association...and time after time returned to the people and land which had captivated his heart.

Currently, as executive director of evangelism with Slavic Gospel Association, Victor returns on a regular basis to the Commonwealth. There he conducts evangelistic crusades--large and small--and evangelism training seminars at the Regional Ministry Centers. Sensitive to Slavic Gospel Association's commitment that we equip and enable the nationals for ministry rather than doing it for them, Victor devotes his energies to teaching evangelists and lay people alike methods of mass evangelism, as well as techniques for one-on-one witnessing.

Churches, athletic stadia, and civic arenas--even places where the lies of Communism and atheism were promulgated on an unsuspecting people--have been filled to overflowing with men and women, boys and girls, hungry for the beautiful and powerful Word of God. Countless thousands have heard and responded to the wondrous story of our Savior's birth, life, death, and resurrection. And, especially exciting is the number of young men burdened with the desire to carry the Good News of God's love to more and more of their own countrymen. These are among those receiving training at the Regional Ministry Center from this very godly man--Victor Branitski.

And, Victor is a visionary. He knows full well, as do many leaders in the national church, that while the door of opportunity remains open, the window of receptivity--the minds and hearts of the people--seems to be closing. It is almost as if there is a glut of religious information. Crowds do not gather quite as readily or in as great numbers as they once did. And yet, Victor is able to see beyond this challenge. Deep within his own heart is the conviction that God's Spirit is still at work empowering many to embrace salvation in Christ. So he presses on untiring and undeterred.

ADDENDUM

U.S. State Department Unclassified Letter

State departmentState Department link https://www.wikileaks.org/plusd/cables/1974MOSCOW13208_b.html

US-SOVIET MARRIAGE: SONTOWSKI-BRANITSKY

Date:1974 August 29, 16:24 (Thursday)

Canonical ID:

1974MOSCOW13208_b

Original Classification:

LIMITED OFFICIAL USE

Current Classification:

UNCLASSIFIED

Handling Restrictions

-- N/A or Blank --

Character Count:

3172

Executive Order:

-- N/A or Blank --

Locator:

TEXT ON MICROFILM,TEXT ONLINE

TAGS:

BRANITSKY, VIKTOR S | CASC - Consular

Concepts:

-- N/A or Blank --

Affairs--Assistance to Citizens | LILLIAN | SONTOWSKI | UR - Soviet Union (USSR) | US - United States

Enclosure: -- N/A or Blank --

Type:

TE - Telegram (cable)

Office Origin:

-- N/A or Blank --

Archive Status:

Electronic Telegrams

Office Action:

ACTION EUR - Bureau of European and Eurasian Affairs

From:

Russia Moscow

Markings:

Declassified/Released US Department of State EO Systematic Review 30 JUN 2005

To: Department of State | Secretary of State

ContentRaw contentMetadataRaw sourcePrintShare

Show Headers

1. FURTHER EVIDENCE OF SOVIET INTRANSIGENCE IN MARRIAGE
AREA IS PROVIDED BY RECENT SOVIET
ACTIONS DESIGNED TO FRUSTRATE

MARRIAGE BETWEEN US CITIZEN LILLIAN
SONTOWSKI AND SOVIET CITIZEN
VIKTOR BRANITSKY OF KIEV.

2. SONTOWSKI AND BRANITSKY APPLIED
FOR MARRIAGE LICENSE AT KIEV
ZAGS OFFICE IN LATE JULY AND RECEIVED
MARRIAGE DATE OF AUGUST 26.
MISS SONTOWSKI, WHO IS ON INTOURIST
TOUR, WAS SCHEDULED TO BE IN
KIEV FROM AUGUST 24 TO 27. HOWEVER,
ON AUGUST 24 KIEV ZAGS
OFFICE RECEIVED SUPPOSEDLY ANONYMOUS
LETTER STATING THAT VIKTOR
BRANITSKY HAD BEEN MENTAL PATIENT IN
VARIOUS KIEV PSYCHIATRIC
HOSPITALS. (DEPT WILL RECALL THAT
SUCH LETTERS HAVE SURFACED
IN PAST MARRIAGE CASES, SUCH AS EPIC
NEMEC-IGNASHEV CASE.)
COUPLE COUNTERED ALLEGATION BY
OBTAINING CERTIFICATE FROM
HOSPITALS MENTIONED IN LETTER TO
EFFECT THAT VIKTOR HAD NEVER
BEEN HOSPITALIZED IN ANY OF THEM.
EVEN THOUGH THIS
APPEARED TO MEET ZAGS REQUIREMENT,
ZAGS OFFICE PUT OFF
MARRIAGE UNTIL AUGUST 31, AND
INTOURIST REFUSED TO EXTEND
SONTOWSKI ITINERARY IN KIEV. MISS
SONTOWSKI ARRIVED

MOSCOW EVENING OF AUGUST 27
ACCOMPANIED BY BRANITSKY.

3. COUPLE BELIEVES, AND CONSOFF
INCLINED TO AGREE, THAT
ZAGS AND INTOURIST ACTION REPRESENTS
ALL TOO FAMILIAR DELIBERATE
LIMITED OFFICIAL USE
LIMITED OFFICIAL USE
PAGE 02 MOSCOW 13208 291812Z

ATTEMPT TO FRUSTRATE US-SOVIET
MARRIAGE PLANS. COUPLE HAS RUN
INTO FURTHER STONEWALL IN MOSCOW, AS
INTOURIST REFUSES TO SELL
MISS SONTOWSKI TICKET TO KIEV. IN
ADDITION, WHEN COUPLE SPOKE
TO KIEV ZAGS BY PHONE FROM MOSCOW
AUGUST 28 IT APPARENT THAT
ALLEGATION OF BRANITSKIY'S SUPPOSED
MENTAL PROBLEMS NOT LAID
TO REST AS COUPLE BELIEVED AND THAT
AUGUST 31 MARRIAGE DATE
MAY NOT BE FIRM.

4. EMBASSY HAS INTERCEDED REPEATEDLY
AT HIGH LEVELS WITH
INTOURIST AND HAS TRANSMITTED
SUPPORTING NOTE TO MFA (Ministry of
Foreign Affairs). HOWEVER,
IN FAMILIAR STYLE, INTOURIST SEEMS TO
BE WORKING DILIGENTLY TO

DISCOVER IMPEDIMENTS RATHER THAN SOLUTIONS TO PROBLEM. REPRESENTATION TO MFA MAY HAVE LITTLE OR NO IMMEDIATE EFFECT. MISS ONTOWSKI'S SOVIET VISA EXPIRES ON SEPTEMBER 2 AND IT SEEMS UNLIKELY SOVIETS WILL ACT TO EXTEND IT. THUS APPEARS THAT, UNLESS SOVIET BUREAUCRATIC STONEWALL SHOULD SUDDENLY CRUMBLE, SONTOWSKI-BRANITSKY MARRIAGE ATTEMPT WILL LIKELY BE FRUSTRATED THIS TIME AND THAT MISS SONTOWSKI MAY LEAVE COUNTRY SEPT 2 WITH UNCERTAIN PROSPECT OF RECEIVING FUTURE SOVIET VISA.

5. COMMENT: COUPLE HAVE SO FAR SHOWN REMARKABLE SANG-FROID (translation from French= cold blood/determination/resolve) IN FACE OF MARRIAGE HASSLE AND SEEM INCLINED TO SEE MATTER THROUGH TO END. THEY HAVE NOT YET CONTACTED WESTERN PRESS ABOUT THEIR PROBLEMS AND HAVE APPARENTLY NO PLANS TO DO SO IN IMMEDIATE FUTURE. HOWEVER, AS DEPT AWARE, AS FRUSTRATIONS MOUNT THIS POSSIBILITY CANNOT BE EXCLUDED.
EXEMPT

STOESSEL
LIMITED OFFICIAL USE
NNN
**References to this document
in other cables**
1974MOSCOW17999

CONTACT INFORMATION

To order a book please go to AMAZON.com

Or for an online PDF with color photos see
https://ia601502.us.archive.org/10/items/from-soviets-to-s
avior/FromSovietsToSavior.pdf

For questions or more information please contact
Victor Branitski.

Email: fromSovietsToSavior@comcast.net

Made in the USA
Columbia, SC
06 November 2020

24085697R00135